INSTANT
INSPIRATION

DOUGIE FORLANO

Next Level

610-715-9664

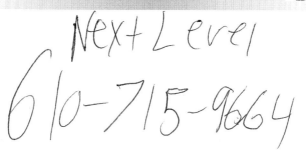

Katie Ball!

Keep Going,
Growing & Glowing

Dougie Forever ♡

THE WISDOM WITHIN

Imagine being able to channel instant inspiration at any given moment, in any given place.

With this book, it's not only possible—it's practical!

Locked away within this book is an alchemist's most valuable tool—a cascade of insight and experience—that will empower you to mold your life into your own beautiful masterpiece. Each page is imparted with an empowering perspective on how you can take simple steps to create stupendous success.

A few years ago, I embarked on an incredible journey where I traveled all over the United States, from the Hollywood Hills of California to the seaport cities of Florida, meeting incredible influencers and absorbing unparalleled wisdom.

Only by Divine agenda or some miraculous force, did I find the willpower to record my experiences, every single day, by creating a series of daily inspirational videos. As I travelled from place to place, I became infused with the intelligence and intuition of many different environments and teachers. Through my videos, I was able to capture some of that wisdom and share it with my vast social media audience. As a result, thousands of people were able to travel with me on my journey - as I worked a miracle of alchemy, transforming my experiences into powerfully packed punches of inspiration every single day.

Today, I have transcribed, revised and optimized these videos for you—in the form of this book to serve as a vehicle for extreme transformation.

Throughout this book—should you choose to invest in it—you will travel with me on my journey to learn all that I have learned. Over the next 365 days, you will absorb the power of my experiences page by page. From Monday through Sunday, for fifty-two weeks straight, you will receive spontaneous sparks of inspiration and wisdom that will sow seeds of success in your life.

As you have most likely already noticed, this book is adorned with an absolutely astounding amount of alliteration. By bedecking this book with back-to-back words that begin with similar sounds, it hammers home the message creating a deeper imprint on your mind. It is bursting with inspiration and will breathe life into you whenever you pick it up. By the way that's what Inspiration means breathe life into something or someone and that someone is you.

Keep it by your bed, in your bathroom, or in your bag. Motivation is like bathing so we need to do it daily to stay ahead and on the ball right?

What lies ahead are 365 dynamic daily guides to drive you to dominate your path to greatness. Each short passage takes less than a minute to read and is the perfect way to be the start to your day. You will get a glance at life through the eyes of someone who was experiencing the most exciting and transformational journey in his lifetime. It will restore

4

your sense of worldly wonderment. As you progress, you will see the world through your own unique and powerful perspective.

The energy within these pages is committed to elevating your mood and enriching your life.

Everyday you get to make a choice: you can choose to see life in a way that will serve you, or in a way that will hold you back. I invite you to read these pages, and week by week, transcend any weakness in your life. It's time to make a choice, bring your limiting beliefs to a halt, and crack open your golden vault of POWER.

With this book you will be vaulting yourself into a place of positive self-talk in a way you may have never tapped into before.

Create a habit of absorbing this content. Treat it as a blessing bestowed on you as your own Divine agenda and I promise it will give you the prophetic power to paint the canvas of your life as you see fit. Habit is where mastery is made.

Practice these techniques, and you will have power in spades.

Take your lemons and make lemonade.

Make sure your shoes are tied tight, because you are about to take flight and step out into the world... a whole new world (Disney voice).

THE JOURNEY

Day 1: Motivated Monday

What do you want to have by the end of this month? Identify your goal and determine what systems and processes will help you reach that goal.

Breakdown:

1. Make a one-month goal.
2. Identify the systems and processes that you will create and act onto achieve that goal.

   IMPORTANT: The systems you create are superior to your goals, because as you will learn later, action is paramount.

Day 2: Thankfulness Tuesday

Feel the absolute exhilaration of being able to talk, to walk, to see, to hear, and to feel. Together, we can appreciate these gifts everyday.

Bring appreciation and awareness to the gifts that you already have! Your body and your health are paramount. Rejoice in that!

Day 3: Wisdom Wednesday

> In *The Theory of Everything*, Stephen Hawking said something that stuck out to me, "intelligence is the ability to adapt to change." So what can you adapt to in your life?

"The only constant is change." What can you bend with, instead of breaking under?

How can you become more accepting of your challenges and move forward with growth? When Stephen Hawking learned he had ALS and a received a tracheotomy, he had to accept and adapt. Doing so allowed him to remain on his extraordinary path!

Be a chameleon and blend with your environment. Be a spider and adjust to the subtle vibrations on your web of social and psychological awareness.

Day 4: Teachability Thursday (In this book we even create new words!)

Are you coachable? Humility is key to progress. Yes, be confident. However, when you couple confidence with receptivity—the willingness to learn and listen—you can accomplish wondrous things.

Find out who's worth listening to and listen—truly listen. Michael Jordan had eleven different coaches at a single point in time.

Steps to receptivity:

1. Ask, "Who can I start learning from?" Double-check their credibility. Make sure they are worth your time and attention.

2. Find people to learn from in several areas in life such as nutrition, fitness, finances, and social skills!

Remember what Dani Johnson said: "Never stop being teachable. If you think you know everything, you will never learn anything."

Day 5: Focus Friday

Today the sun will shine on us all.

Do you know the most interesting fact about the sun's energy? It is brought to focus through our atmosphere. What can you concentrate on with precision and accuracy today?

Be like a camera and focus on what's great!

Remember, "The successful warrior is the average man, with laser-like focus." – Bruce Lee

Day 6: Superhero Saturday

Are you a superwoman? Are you a superman? What's your super power— your skill, your strength?

How can you stupendously, sensationally share it with the world?

Identify it, recognize it, and use it to contribute. Use your skills, build on your strengths and serve others with them.

....

Day 7: Service Sunday

The secret to supporting yourself is serving others. Today, give any emotion that you wish to experience to someone else! In return, it will automatically come back to you. It's magic and makes you feel ecstatic, so make it a habit, and hop to it today like a rabbit.

How can you serve yourself and someone else today? When you serve somebody else you become the source of what you want. You become the sorcerer. A sorcerer is abundantly resourceful—so serve!

> "Find yourself by losing yourself in the service of others." – Gandhi

....

Day 8: Masterpiece Monday

Are you crafting your life like an artist would craft a sculpture? Are you chipping away every single day to reveal your vision as reality? Or do you have a *lottery ticket mentality* where you expect the fulfillment of your desires right away, and you are not willing to work for them?

Today, I encourage you to see the beauty in the long game. Make your life into a sculpture, a masterpiece. Begin to work hard today, so you can reap the reward tomorrow. The process might not be sexy, but the end result certainly will be!

Getting that bod, mastering your career, and earning your millions all starts with one small action today.

Day 9: Thankfulness Tuesday

There are a million things to be thankful for. Your body is healthy and whole. Your heart is drumming life through your veins. The light surrounds you. Take a moment to think of four things you're grateful for. Reflect on four things of which you're infinitely appreciative. Fully feel that appreciation.

Think of at least four gems that deserve your gratitude, right now. Go!

Day 10: Why Me? Wednesday

You are unique. There will never be another *you*.

> "You have to be odd to be number one." – Dr. Seuss

How can you stand out? By being fully and authentically yourself. Own who you are and your individuality will shine. Strive for greatness and you will stand out among the pack. Better yourself and become your best. The purple cow will always be the most interesting in the herd.

Elevate, escalate, and levitate yourself.

"To be great is to be misunderstood." – Ralph Waldo Emerson

ACTION STEP: Force yourself out of your comfort zone and do at least one outrageous thing today.

....

Day 11: Thankfulness Thursday

I regularly realize that I really appreciate that I'm a great student and not a follower.

Are you a student or a follower?

Be grateful that you can learn from others and then apply that knowledge in a way that you see fit.

....

Day 12: Fountain Friday

The Roman emperor Marcus Aurelius said, "Look within. Within is the fountain of good. It will bubble up if you dig." Dig in your mind and heart, and watch the greatness that emerges from it today.

....

Day 13: Standard Saturday

Once I changed my standards, things drastically changed. Raise your standards. . If you do, you will notice that certain things become unacceptable—including others' behaviors and your own. For greater results, elevate to greater standards!

....

Day 14: Skyline Sunday

Create a beautiful layout for your goals. Then, define your approach for achieving those goals. Line them up for the week ahead, then execute on them.

....

Day 15: Make Things Happen Monday

TGIM! Since Monday is my favorite day of the week, I have something special for you. There are three types of people in this world—

1. Those that watch things happen

2. Those that wonder what will happen

3. Those that make things happen

Today, I want you to focus on being the third type of person. It's OK to watch, to observe, and to learn. However, you must not forget to act! Without action, life will slip through your fingers and you will end up wondering what could have been. Ultimately, the goal is to be the executor—the dominator! No fapping, napping, slacking or lollygagging

Get it cracking.

Make it happen, Captain.

Day 16: Totally Tuesday

When you are absolutely, positively, 100% committed to something, the answers always come. So what are you totally all-in on?

Day 17: Wisdom Wednesday

> Billionaire, Warren Buffett, suggests, "You can only learn from mistakes."

However, they don't have to be your mistakes. It's a heck of alot easier to learn from the mistakes of others. Whose mistakes can you learn from? How can learning from others' mistakes help you avoid some of your own?

Learn from the failures of others through books, mentors, classes, coaches, and videos. If you wish, ask other people to share their experiences. You can save yourself years of mistakes and accomplish your goals infinitely faster.

> "You must learn from mistakes of others. You can't possibly live long enough to make them all yourself."
> – Sam Levenson

Day 18: Thrive Thursday

Let's challenge ourselves to become our absolute best and actualize our potential. Commit to a thriving mindset and to living from moment to moment. Trust me, today will be fun.

Every day you have the choice to merely cope and survive or to step out of that mindset and live on your edge. Get up, rise, be fully alive, and touch the sky.

If you are not living at your edge, you are taking up too much space.

Day 19: Faith Friday

Today, the sun will rise. Maybe it already has.

That sun will rise every single morning.

> Mother Theresa said, "Faith keeps the person who keeps the faith." Have faith that your life will unfold how you see fit. See your success before you have it. Feed your faith and starve your doubts.

Forget fear. Flush it out. Fear will fade in the intense light of trust and gratitude.

> "Promise me that you'll always remember, you are braver than you believe, stronger than you seem, and smarter than you think." – Christopher Robin

Day 20: Stellar Saturday

Life is an epic journey where you can glow, glisten, and gleam like the city lights, and shine and sparkle like the stars.

Both the natural and unnatural world can shine so bright. Identify something that is both natural and unnatural for you to do today that will get you closer to your goals. Take action on both of those things.

Day 21: Cold Shower Sunday

Want to get in the habit of turning "I can't" into "I must?" Start by stepping out of your comfort zone. Next time you experience hesitation about doing something, train your brain to push past it.

A great, practical way to step outside of your comfort zone is to take a freezing-cold shower. It will make you braver and will build your "courage muscles." If you're looking for ways to toughen up, this is the trick. Be brave and brazen. Mess with your own head. It will subconsciously train your mind to step out of your comfort zone more often.

Some other comfort-zone challenges are:

1. Sleep less
2. Skip a meal
3. Don't use your phone for a day
4. Talk to 15 new girls or guys
5. Be more generous
6. Skip sugar for the day

Get creative! Life can be challenging. Eliminate the softness. Create high-level toughness! Build your "courage muscles," and it will serve you.

Day 22: Mash It Up Monday

Mash up your fears, your insecurities, and your doubts. Destroy, devour, and disintegrate them. Fear is mainly False Evidence Appearing Real!

Lao Tzu said, "There is no illusion greater than fear." Smash your fears into smithereens!

"Men are not afraid of things but how they view them." – Epictetus

"The only thing we have to fear is fear itself." – Franklin D Roosevelt

"Always do what you are afraid to do." – Ralph Waldo Emerson

You got this!

Day 23: Thankfulness Tuesday

Flip a switch and there's light. Press a button and there's music. Turn a knob and there's water. We are gifted with so many tools that help make life easier. Take a moment to acknowledge that.

Remember, many of these gifts did not exist years ago and even more will exist tomorrow. Let's rejoice in the abundance of blessings!

Today, open the window and wish the sky, the birds, and the sun a good morning. Light, music, and water are all instantly accessible. That's so exciting!

Day 24: Wisdom Wednesday

Jim Rohn, the great businessman and philosopher, has said, "Don't wish it were easier, wish you were better."

By improving myself, I have improved my life. All it took was a simple shift in my paradigm. You, too, can become more aware of your shortcomings and self. Cultivating awareness can transform your life.

"Don't wish for less problems wish for more skills. Don't wish for less challenges wish for more wisdom."
– Jim Rohn

Day 25: Triumph Thursday

The difference between "try," and "triumph," is that little bit of "umph."

When your back is against the wall, you have to tap into that super-you. Awaken the best version of yourself. Get in a state of mind that will empower you. Find ways to access that incredible flow state. There is brilliance in resilience.

When you are faced with a deadline at the last minute, do you focus and rise to the occasion? It takes courage, but experiment to find out what makes you tick.

This is elite level stuff.

"I learned that courage was not the absence of fear, but the TRIUMPH over it. The brave man is not he who does not feel afraid, but he who conquers that fear." – Nelson Mandela

Remember that the difference between "try," and "triumph," is that little bit of "umph."

....

Day 26: Feeling Fresh Friday

I love to spend time in the library—particularly in the audiobooks section. Books allow me to get a fresh insight on life.

Everyone has different experiences and perspectives on life. The abundance of books in the library allows you to absorb all of those valuable insights. Fill up on the good stuff.

As a bonus, here is simple, secret strategy to learn at an incredible rate: go on Youtube and listen to audiobooks you are interested in for free. Absorb others' insight while you are on the go and cut the learning curve. This is a lethal weapon to make you more creative, constructive and cerebral in your cerebellum.

Day 27: Smarten Up Saturday

The best things in life are found on the top shelf. Health, wealth, mansions, cool cars, a winning team, love and joy are sitting high, but they are within reach. Each book that you read can serve as a ladder rung, a freaking stepping stone on your journey to attaining all the things you want on the top shelf.

Leaders are readers. Knowledge will elevate your game and place you closer to your goals. To succeed, you must read!

"The book you don't read won't help." – Jim Rohn

Day 28: Step Up Sunday

In which area of your life can you step up the most? Is it health, wealth, love, happiness, work, or school?

Discover where you can grow and double down on making it happen. Step up!

"The ladder of success is best climbed by stepping on the rungs of opportunity." – Ayn Rand

Identify an area for improvement and focus on really crushing it this week.

Day 29: Make It Happen Monday

I once believed that knowledge is power. It's not. *Applied* knowledge is power.

"Just do it," like Nike.

> Remember, "some people want it to happen, some wish it would happen, others make it happen."
> – Michael Jordan

....

Day 30: Thankfulness Tuesday

A great way to skyrocket your happiness is to keep a gratitude journal.

To create a gratitude journal, write down what you're grateful in a book three to five times a day. Charge the book with the feeling of pure appreciation and watch your quality of life explode.

Don't ever leave home without your journal! In my experience, it only took two weeks of gratitude journaling to feel super wealthy, healthy, and blessed.

The science is out! It definitely helps. I wish I did it sooner! I bet you will too.

> "I would maintain that thanks are the highest form of thought; and gratitude is happiness doubled by wonder." – G.K. Chesterton

Day 31: Wisdom Wednesday

> Warren Buffett says, "The more you learn, the more you earn."

> Equally as important, Benjamin Franklin said, "An investment in knowledge pays the best interest."

I admire those creators, so I take their advice.

In fact, I have been taking their advice and guess what? It's working. I have never met anybody who regretted reading or learning too much. However, I do hear many express that wish they knew something that other people do.

Whom do you aspire to be like? Are they worth listening to? How will you manage to learn from them?

Day 32: Thankfulness Thursday

At this very moment, people are crossing the ocean— attempting to immigrate to the United States. If you live in a first world country, you have an abundance of opportunities. Let's recognize our blessings and maximize our outstanding advantages. Squeeze the most out of every opportunity like toothpaste.

> "Give thanks for a little and you will find a lot."
> – Hausa

Day 33: Future Friday

To get to the other end of the bridge (your end goal) you have to do what it takes. So first you must ask yourself, do you know what it takes?

Then, determine if you are willing to do it.

> "Discipline is the bridge between goals and accomplishment." – Jim Rohn

> "The Future depends on what we do in the present." – Gandhi

Find out the price you have to pay. Resolve to pay that price no matter what.

Day 34: Shine Saturday

Have you ever been to Times Square in New York City? It's big, bright and beautiful—just like I want you to be. When you shine, you inspire others. You let them shine.

> Barry Woods says, "So sparkle and shine." The moment we let go of our fears and express ourselves, we empower others to do the same.

Get your shine on!

Day 35: Serenity Sunday

Through presence and acceptance you will find peace and comfort. That is the process. Embody it.

> As expressed in The Serenity Prayer, "God grant me the serenity to accept the things I cannot change, the courage to change the things I can; and the wisdom to know the difference."

There is no fun in the future. Fun is found along the journey.

....

Day 36: March Up Monday

Life is tough sometimes. It can be an uphill battle. Sometimes you have to battle your way all the way to the top. Burst up, give it everything you got and life can still deal you tremendous blows.

The quality of your life is determined by how you respond to those challenges. How will you respond?

I invite you to enjoy the battles, to be grateful for them, and learn from them. Let pain propel you forward and upward. Burst, explode, and erupt! Ride the upward spiral to success.

....

Day 37: Tap Dance to Work Tuesday

You must have passion and excitement for your career. It's essential if you want to optimize your health, your wealth, your love, and your life.

Discover meaning in what you do. If you cannot discover it, create it. If you can't create it, fake it. Fake it until you make it.

Are you fired up about your career?

Here are some *action tips* if you aren't feeling it:

1. Make a plan to transition to a more fruitful job.
2. Create a purpose while you are there. Find ways to make it exciting. Challenge yourself to make it fun and contribute.
3. Adopt a side project that truly lights you up and fulfills you. When the time is right and you have accumulated enough resources, dive in and fully commit.
4. Seek more guidance, advice, and leadership.
5. Experiment to discover the best avenue to share your gifts and build an abundant lifestyle.

Day 38: Wisdom Wednesday

"Yesterday is history. Tomorrow is a mystery. Today is a gift, that's why we call it the present." - Bill Keane

Stomp on your limiting beliefs about the past and the future. Live in the here and now. The past does not dictate the future. Let go of guilt, avoid resistance, surrender your identity, and don't seek salvation in the future. Accept what is and simply be.

"Become aware of just how rarely your attention is truly in the now. Knowing that you are not present is a great success. That knowing is presence."
– Eckhart Tolle

Make friends with this moment!

....

Day 39: Thankfulness Thursday

Throughout my childhood, I always dreamed of going to Muscle Beach in Venice, CA. I was super-duper blessed to visit recently and even found time to get a workout in. Throughout my childhood I always imagined going there, and I made that happen.

What did you want to do in this world? What have you done? Are you grateful for it? How can you be?

Explore! I challenge you to expand, because it's your Divine right.

....

Day 40: Fetch Friday

Chase after one thing and one thing only: your dream. Go after it like a dog chasing a stick. Then come back and inspire others to do the same and, like a dog , let's have fun as we do it.

Day 41: Spring-Fever Saturday Goal Setting

Let's supercharge ourselves and set some goals! What do you want to accomplish in six months, in one month, by the end of the week?

What processes and systems will you focus on, execute, and dominate? Are you on course to accomplish those goals?

Set your alarm for fifteen minutes. Write down a minimum of ten goals for the month. Pick your top three! Then, most importantly, create the systems and processes thatwill allow you to accomplish those goals.

When you have completed the exercise, find some trusted people to hold you accountable.

Go!

· ·

Day 42: Set Goals Sunday

A friend of mine, Adam Farfan, became a teenage millionaire. He retired at age 24. He believes Sunday is the best day to actually set your goals for the whole week.

Set yourself up for success. Write down where you want to go. Write down what you want to do. Write down what you want to achieve, eat, see, share, and be.

> "Set your goals high and don't stop until you get there." – Bo Jackson

"I focus on my goals and try to ignore the rest."
– Venus Williams

"Life takes on meaning when you become motivated, set goals and charge after them in an unstoppable manner." – Les Brown

"Manage Activity and Focus on Results (MAFR)!"
– Adam Farfan

Day 43: Malibu Most Wanted Monday

How can you be the most wanted in your career and relationships? Desirability is a great skill to cultivate. Become attractive by being an attractive person.

Day 44: Tow Truck Tuesday

Say goodbye to the beliefs and ideas that don't serve and support you. Most of them were likely formed unconsciously. They are items of the past. Tow them away. Start to cultivate positive beliefs consciously from now on.

Day 45: Wisdom Wednesday

Procrastination is the worst nation on planet Earth. So early in the morning, I like to write my number one goal for the day. From there, it's just execution.

What's your number one goal today?

....

Day 46: Thankfulness Thursday

Have you ever been in a life or death situation? How did you feel after you got out OK?

I was once hit by car while riding my bike. It was a terrifying experience.Fortunately, I made it out OK. I was grateful for helping hands and for my life itself. It put things in perspective. I had my helmet on, and realized after the incident how blessed I am to have protected my most important asset that allows us to creatively express ourselves... because your brain is your most important asset. It allows you to creatively express yourself.

What are you absolutely blessed for? Flood yourself with gratitude and share it with others. Celebrate what you appreciate!

....

Day 47: Fail Friday

How do you respond to failure?

If you dream big, you need a positive perspective on failure.

Failure can be a resource—a tool that you can use to grow. You can fail forward while learning and growing. You can accept failure as a lesson or you can let it define you. Which will you choose?

"Failure is an event, not a person." – Zig Ziglar

"When we succeed, we party. When we fail, we ponder." – Tony Robbins

"Failure is not fatal, but failure to change might be."
– John Wooden

Failure can be a resource—a tool that you can use to grow. You can fail forward while learning and growing. You can accept failure as a lesson or you can let it define you. Which will you choose?

Day 48: Smash Saturday

Think of a limiting belief that you have. Maybe you believe you suck at math, you can't cook, or you can't go to the gym. Identify that barrier and smash it! Crush the and excuses with discipline. I can think of a thousand excuses why I won't succeed that could deter me from moving forward; but, I refuse to buy into them. Please, do the same for yourself!

> "Nothing is impossible; there are ways that lead to everything, and if we had sufficient WILL we should always have sufficient means. It is often merely for an excuse that we say things are impossible."
> – La Rochefoucauld

Day 49: Share Sunday

Can you add more water to a glass that is already full? Yes, you can.

All you have to do is pour some water out into another glass. Then you will have the space to fill it again. When you share, you have the opportunity to learn more. You can learn deeper and more fully. When you share ideas, emotions, experiences, etc., you invite other things to come back to you. *You* create the space for more insight.

Have the courage to share and welcome the ability to receive. The glass will magically grow taller and taller allowing you to serve and learn more. The growth is incredibly infinite!

Day 50: Momentum Monday

Muster up momentum like a bicycle rolling down a hill. Momentum is powerful.

Ride that bicycle (momentum) until the wheels fall off! Keep going! Sometimes it's tough to get started, but once the hard part is over the magnificence of momentum takes control. What simple action could you take today to produce new momentum that will propel you towards success in your life?

Day 51: Time Tuesday

Steve Jobs of Apple suggested that time is one of your most valuable resources. Don't waste it working for someone else's vision. Take action for *your* dreams and goals today.

> "Your time is limited, so don't waste it living someone else's life. Don't be trapped by dogma-which is living with the results of other people's thinking. Don't let the noise of other's opinions drown out your own inner voice. And most important, have the courage to follow your heart and intuition." – Steve Jobs

> "We cannot teach people anything. We can only help them reveal it in themselves." – Galileo

Remember that greatness already resides within you. Today, I will assist you in awakening it.

....

Day 52: Windup Wednesday

Start your engine and floor it.

Discover your dreams, and visualize them well. Then windup, and burst, blast, and erupt towards your goals.

....

Day 53: Track Thursday

If you don't stay on track, you will delay your dream life. Focus on your path—even when it is raining—even when it is dark.

If you are facing a challenging time in your life, maintain focus. Remember, what matters most: your purpose.

Day 54: Fear Friday

The opposite of success is not failure; it's fear. How do you eliminate your doubts to make the fear disappear? With awareness, gratitude, courage and massive radical action. So cultivate awareness, be grateful, and have the courage to take massive action today.

Day 55: Success Saturday

I define success as progressive realization and progress towards worthy goals. What is it for you? How do you define it?

> Jim Rohn said, "Success is nothing more than a few disciplines repeated every day."

The point is to focus on process not on the outcome. Oddly enough, when you do that, you end up producing a better outcome.

Day 56: Shadow Sunday

Have you ever noticed how big your shadow can appear in the early morning? That's how truly big we really are.

We are larger than we believe. We are beautifully big. Know your true size. Live like it. Act like it. Be like it!

Our potential is huge, enormous, Jurassic, mammoth! Too often we wake as lions but act like mice. Wake up and smell your excellence!

Day 57: Magnificent Monday

It is a magnificent, marvelous, miraculous, Monday. Why do I believe this Monday will be so great? Because of the attitude I bring to life. When people ask me how I'm doing, I say "outstanding, stupendous, terrific." It brings a zest to my day and spices up my approach to life.

So how are you doing?

> "Your attitude, not your aptitude, will determine your altitude." – Zig Ziglar

A shift in your mindset is a small change that will make a big difference. Take responsibility for your attitude, create it and choose—as you always have the ability to do—where to direct your focus. Bring pure positivity, and focus on the most meaningful priority.

Day 58: Tie-It-Together Tuesday

If you love and want the best for yourself, then meditate. When you meditate, you can serve the world from a better place. When you serve from that place, you free your mind and free yourself from things that are holding you back.

The most selfless thing you can do is meditate.

Day 59: Wisdom Wednesday

The key to life is that there is no key. It's a combination. Life is a combination. It's a process of figuring things out one turn at a time.

There's no key to success. When you resonate with that, you will find peace.

Day 60: Thankfulness Thursday

Be conscious of your gifts. Rejoice in your treasures. Be happy with what have, while you pursue everything that you desire.

"If you count all your assets, you will always show a profit." – Robert Quillen

Day 61: Full Engagement Friday

If you are only going to give 90%, then you might as well not even try. Give 100%, all the time. It is the most fulfilling, rewarding experience. Give your best or don't give anything at all. Go hard or go home.

If your tired or sick and you only have 85% today, then give 100% of that 85%.

> "Under any circumstance, simply do your best and you will avoid self-judgment, abuse and regret."
> – Don Miguel Ruiz

> "You can still do your best." – Sean Combs

Give all of yourself today. Your future self will thank you.

....

Day 62: Soaked Saturday

Drench yourself in wonderful, positive ideas.

Don't waste the ideas that come up. Absorb them because they can be brilliant leaps or small productive steppingstones. Get in the habit of tracking your ideas and acting on them immediately.

> "Motivation is when you get a hold of an idea, inspiration is when an idea gets a hold of you."
> – Dr. Wayne Dyer

....

Day 63: Sweep Sunday

Sweep up your positive thoughts and put them into action.

What are some of your phenomenal ideas?

Have the courage to implement them. Let this Sunday serve as a broom of bravery, sweeping all your aspirations into action. Remember, you have plenty of resources to turn your dreams into reality.

Day 64: Magician Monday

Ask how you can serve others with your negative experiences? Benefit from everything and change the meaning of it. You have the magic power to turn those lessons into blessings, tests into testimonies, your mess into a message.

"Leaders must invoke an alchemy of great vision"
– Henry Kissinger

Become an opportunistic optimizing optimist. Be a wizard. Be an alchemist. Turn a negative into a positive. Everything you touch can turn to gold. If something bad happens in your life, transform it into something empowering. Make a lesson out of it.

Day 65: Tool Belt Tuesday

Let's get some tools in your tool belt. A soldier with a well-equipped tool belt is ready for battle. To be a warrior in life, get strapped with skills and preparation.

Add the skills you need and be prepared to use them.

"Prepare when it's easy." – Lao Tzu

Day 66: Wisdom Wednesday

> "Will you look back on life and say, 'I wish I had,' or 'I'm glad I did?'" – Zig Zigler

Answer that question. Don't neglect to reflect and determine if the path you're on is one that you decided to take—not one forced on you by someone else.

Follow your own heart and intuition.

· ·

Day 67: Thankfulness Thursday

Everyday I am deeply appreciative for the opportunities I have. One of the best abundant opportunities I have is the ability to practice random acts of kindness. I can create them everywhere. They are an opportunity that anyone can create.

Every moment, you can be kind.

> George Saunders said in his famous commencement speech, "What I regret most in my life are failures of kindness."

· ·

Day 68: Firework Friday

You want to make noise in life? You want be witnessed even from a distance? Then be like a firework and burst, blast and erupt. Get your sparkle on.

Bring the heat the rest of the week! Finish school or work with some loud power. Catalyze the momentum that comes from explosive action and accomplishment. The fire inside you works. Use it like a firework. When you do, you'll be seen and heard from far away.

....

Day 69: Study Saturday

Let's double down on the books. You don't have to be in school to study. Study in life. I share the wisdom of Stephen Covey. Whose wisdom do you share?

Life gives us tests, which serve as opportunities to become students of the world.

"Success depends upon prior preparation."– Confucius

REMINDER: Put the time and grind in. Test your toughness and tenacity.

....

Day 70: Slice It Sunday

Sometimes it seems like success is locked away behind an impenetrable door. To discover what's behind that door, break the lock through the power of reading.

Anyway you slice it, to get past that door you must read. Reading creates the health, wealth, love, and happiness effect! Not only does it give knowledge, it builds focus and strengthens willpower by working out the prefrontal cortex.

Your mind is muscle. Exercise it daily, not rarely. Break the habit of not reading, and start now!

Day 71: Magnetic Monday

The law of attraction is a powerful tool. Implement it. Essentially, it suggests that your most dominant thoughts will attract your reality. So shift your focus from the negative to the positive. And don't forget the last thing. Take action!

> "Once you make a decision, the universe conspires to make it happen." – Ralph Waldo Emerson

> "You are the Michelangelo of your own life. The David that you are sculpting is you and you do it with your thoughts." – Joe Vitale

> "A man is but the product of his thoughts. What he thinks he becomes." – Gandhi

> "As you think, so shall you become." – Bruce Lee

Like attracts like. Fully believe in yourself then take action on your deepest desires.

Day 72: Tipping Tuesday

My buddy Ken Rochon wrote fourteen books, emphasizing the importance of persistence. If you actually put in the time, you will automatically become an expert. It is human nature.

He proves that it's not luck or skill. It's hard work.

Keep moving in a consistent direction and eventually all your hard work will tip over into tremendous achievement.

Trust in that and keep moving!

....

Day 73: Wisdom Wednesday

Ralph Waldo Emerson said, "God will not have his work made manifest by cowards." How will you be bold, brave, and brazen today as you move forward?

Show some moxie today.

....

Day 74: Thankfulness Thursday

I'm so blessed with the ability to travel. Think about it... we have easy access to planes, trains, cars, and buses. We can go wherever we want to go. So explore, adventure, and travel. Express your gratitude for the ease of exploring new places.

....

Day 75: Flytrap Friday

When a fly lands on a Venus flytrap, the flytrap snaps and grabs it. How can we be like Venus flytraps? When an opportunity comes our way, how can we snap and grab it before the opportunity to nourish ourselves has passed us by?

Day 76: Sign Saturday

Everyday people are erecting signs on the road, on billboards, and on buildings telling us what to do and where to buy. We need to erect some signs in our own life to remind ourselves to adopt habits and take actions that will serve us. What would your billboard say?

. . . .

Day 77: Sleep Sunday

We all know sleep is essential.

> "Early to bed, Early to rise, Makes you Healthy, Wealthy, and Wise." – Ben Franklin

Start good practices like reading and journaling before going to sleep, which help you enjoy a better night's sleep.

. . . .

Day 78: Mystical Monday

Believe in mermaids. Believe in Santa Claus. Believe in heaven. It doesn't really matter. Perception is reality, so enjoy the duality and believe in things that serve and support you.

. . . .

Day 79: Tree Tuesday

I once saw a tree that has been alive since 1910, and to this day, is still growing fruit. It's amazing. How can we live as long as these trees and continue to be fruitful?

Think about your health.

Day 80: Wisdom Wednesday

We do what we feel.

A Moritist maxim says, "Behavior wags the tail of feelings."

In other words, feelings follow behavior. So act calm and you will be calm. Act happy and you will be happy. Don't allow your tail to wag you.

Day 81: Thankfulness Thursday

If you're not grateful for all the great gifts around you, it is unlikely that you will receive more of them. Remember, *what you appreciate, appreciates.*

Day 82: Friends Friday

Show me your friends, and I will show you your future. Be a friend to have a friend. Remember, the best friendships are the ones that are unexpected.

Day 83: Save Saturday

I was once a lifeguard and I saved a lot of lives, but my new purpose is to save lives through this book and my YouTube videos. This is a repurposed way for me to continue saving lives. I get to save people from going down that downward spiral of unfounded rationalizations, quitting, depression, and hopelessness.

How are you able to save people in your life?

Day 84: Stupendous Sunday

Do you ever have to pinch yourself to realize where you are and see how beautiful life is? It's amazing to have new experiences and meet new awesome people. Revel in that beauty of new relationships and natural beauty today.

Day 85: Mix-It-Up Monday

Life is constantly moving. It never stops. It's never static. Accept the truth of change instead of grasping onto things. Beware of just going with the flow of others and the environment.

Today, jump into the current of life and swim with it for maximum speed. Only dead fish go with the flow. Instead, go against the current. Dictate your direction and build massive momentum deliberately, proactively and passionately.

Being dynamic, skilled, flexible and spontaneous will serve you stupendously on this planet.

Be ready and alert to change so you can snag opportunities. Following the same patterns will never allow you to do that.

Day 86: Twirl Tuesday

Your surroundings can help or hurt you depending on how you respond to them.

It all depends on your resourcefulness, creativity, focus, mindset, sensitivity, appreciation and what you do with the brilliance that surrounds you in every moment.

Learn to be a chef of life. Craft amazing things out of a variety of ingredients. Practice awareness and alchemy and you'll become unstoppable, because no matter what life throws at you, you can always create greatness out of it.

Use the environment to your advantage.

Day 87: Wisdom Wednesday

"Success depends upon previous preparation, and without such preparation there is sure to be failure."
– Confucius

However, don't wait until you are ready to start.

I've found, as many others also have, you don't have to be 100% ready to jump into action. Colin Powell says all it takes is 40%.

So what are you waiting for? Either act now or start preparing today!

> So many people prepare, get set and aim before they fire. In truth, you should fire then aim. Be prepared and remember, "You don't have to be great to start but you have to start to be great." – Zig Ziglar

Day 88: Thankfulness Thursday

I'm grateful for my friend @hugejoshman, who can make the tastiest, yummiest, and most colorful meals.

His dishes are second to none. Super healthy too! He provides all the essential nutrients, veggies, fats and proteins to fuel people to perform optimally throughout the day.

Every morning his breakfast hits the spot like a polka dot.

On top of that, like me, he is a Philadelphia Eagles fanatic.

God can place the perfect people in your life when you become appreciative of who is already there.

He can also put some savory scrumptious food there too, if you treat your blessings with joy and gratitude.

Day 89: Foundation Friday

Do you have a strong, solid foundation? If you don't follow the fundamentals of life, career, health and relationships, don't expect lasting success.

Strong houses are built on a strong foundation. Trust me, this comes from experience. I've had the rug ripped out from right under me numerous times because I did not abide to the basics.

Continuously reflect on the values and rules you have set in your life. You have decided to live by these values. Share them with people you love, the activities you engage in and in everyday life.

Build your life upon rock rather than sand to avoid collapsing when challenges arise.

Day 90: Snag Saturday

I once scored a tremendous touchdown while playing some beach football.

However, the most epic part was the touchdown dance.

Preparation plus opportunity equals luck. Years of watching football, playing pick up games with friends, great cardio, and an excellent throw (aka opportunity) allowed me to make that catch. Optimizing my speed, hand eyed coordination, and trusting my faculties allowed me to execute.

 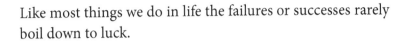
Like most things we do in life the failures or successes rarely boil down to luck.

Day 91: Shop Sunday

I was up in the Hollywood Hills watching people shop for foods and goods at the farmers market. However, you can also shop for skills.

By investing time and money into books, hiring a great coach, attending classes, seminars and trainings you skyrocket your abilities.

Skill acquisition is the smartest shopping that we can do.

> "Every skill you acquire doubles your odds for success." – Scott Adams

Day 92: Motion Monday

One of my personal rules of life is to never go through the motions of my day. I want my actions to be meaningful.

I must live with a powerful presence of passion and purpose.

How about you? Are you unconsciously moving through your day, your job, your classes or your workouts?

How can you add some meaning, life, zeal and zest to your actions?

Day 93: Turn Tuesday

"Activity finishes the miracle process of turning nothing into something." – Jim Rohn

In my success tracker, I ask myself these three questions:

1. How can I mold my knowledge, ideas, skills and emotions into value?
2. What will I focus on being today?
3. What will I focus on doing today?

These questions support me sensationally.

Day 94: Wisdom Wednesday

"God will not have his work made manifest by cowards." – Ralph Waldo Emerson

When you take the call to adventure and embark on a hero's journey, you will have to fight big ugly fire-breathing dragons—not sidestep tiny lizards. The dragons are your challenges.

What is something deep down that you know you should stop doing?

What is something deep down you know should start doing?

These are your dragons. Take a deep breath, and appreciate the audacity you will muster to face these challenges.

Day 95: Thankfulness Thursday

Do you appreciate nature?

Whenever I become present with nature and let go of my thoughts, I experience true appreciation.

The Power of Now by Eckhart Tolle is an amazing book that helped me get in touch with this blessing.

> "Have you ever gazed up into the infinity of space on a clear night, awestruck by the absolute stillness and inconceivable vastness of it? Have you listened, truly listened, to the sound of the mountain stream in the Forrest?" – Eckhart Tolle.

These gifts of nature are always available to us.

Day 96: Fertilizer Friday

> "Failure is good. It's fertilizer. Everything I've learned about coaching, I've learned from making mistakes."
> – Rick Pitino

In my experience, the tough times I have endured now serve as meaningful blessings. They have shaped and inspired me.

Today, I know with conviction that challenges only help me grow stronger.

Be resilient and empower yourself.

Day 97: Superficial Saturday

I like to dig deep down into the rabbit holes of life. They help me learn, become surprised, and become more inspired.

Whenever I dig beneath the superficial layers, I am shocked by what I discover. By digging deeper, you can uncover a world of things that you might not understand yet.

Be grateful whenever you get a glimpse of things in a deeper or different light. Invite curiosity and fascination. Learn more and immediately apply your knowledge through experimentation. As you go deep down to the bottom, you will find truth and meaning.

....

Day 98: Spiritual Sunday

Activate your potentiality! Radiate from the inside instead of reacting from the outside. Expand your excellence.

This life is for you. It wants you to be successful! Don't block your blessings.

Behave from your best vibration because you have it all.

Today's *action tip:* Agree with three people on the awesomeness of life. Avoid complaining.

Embrace your intrinsic, electric, titanic, dynamic, infinite spirit.

Day 99: Mature Monday

As you grow, know that you are advancing and sharpening in your own way.

The flower that has not fully bloomed is still radiating with aliveness and potential. People may say you're too young or too old. However, that's their limiting belief. You do not have to accept that as an excuse. You can still thrive and excel. Don't accept others' limitations. Go for what you want, when you want it.

You are exactly where you are supposed to be in your development. Everything is in perfect order, even the timing! However, take expedited action to accelerate your maturity. Be in a rush, but not in a hurry.

Enjoy and smell the roses on your run, but remember that your purpose is to run. Humility comes with maturity.

....

Day 100: Technology Tuesday

I would not be able to make my videos if it wasn't for technology. Technology is evolving at a rapid rate and it will only develop faster.

We must use it wisely—filtering out what does not serve us and leveraging what helps grow. Make life less arduous and increase opportunities. Most of all leave a better imprint and contribute to the world!

Day 101: Wisdom Wednesday

Just learned a new tool. Honestly though, I was hesitant before I implemented it.

Despite my hesitation, I plunged in and committed to it 100%. Once, I did I completed the task with ease.

I took action, and it felt amazing. I even celebrated when I finished. Then this quote popped into my head:

"Inspiration does exist but it must find you working."
– Pablo Picaso

"Whatever you can do, or dream you can, begin it. Boldness has genius, power and magic in it."
– Jonathan von Goethe

Day 102: Thankfulness Thursday

One night, as we were hanging out in the kitchen, Ryan Clarkin, Mark Dhamma and I gave each other feedback on our individual strengths and weaknesses!

Colossal growth comes from feedback! Through feedback you can learn what is and isn't working from another person's perspective.

Plus, you can surrender your ego for a moment. It feels amazing.

"Feedback, is not only opportunity to massively grow, it's an opportunity to lose your ego." – Ryan Clarkin

Feedback we need that.

Day 103: Fulfilling Friday

You will experience utmost enjoyment when you are being the person that you truly want to be.

Write that down.

Then describe that person. Make it your mission to become and live like that individual. That is the highest version of you.

Acting and behaving like the person you want to be, will inspire you.

Day 104: Seminar Saturday

Lewis Howes hosted one of the most extraordinary events I have ever attended. He created an incredible learning experience that went well above and beyond what was expected.

I go to at least six seminars a year to invest in myself.

How often do you seek out perspective from people who are at the top? I encourage you to invest in yourself because you are worth it. Find a way to invest in yourself today.

"To be authentic means you are in the moment. And to be in the moment requires preparation. So preparation and improvisation will produce spontaneity. Improvisation without preparation, is winging it.-Michael Port

Day 105: Scale Up Sunday

A little more than four years before I wrote this book, I hit rock bottom.

Ever since then, I have decided I want better for myself and have become committed to living a life of higher standards. As a result, my growth has been insurmountable. My experiences have been extraordinary. My relationships have been priceless. My potential has been realized. It is breathtaking!

I will continue to climb high and enjoy the rise to the top. I deeply wish the same for you too!

Day 106: Magical Monday

To achieve wealth, health, happiness, and love you must simply implement habit and action on a consistent basis.

Success is not a spooky, mysterious, or even genetic gift. We are entitled to it.

Understand, though, success isn't something you "get." It's something you do and be.

Remember what Jim Rohn said, "Success is simply a few disciplines practiced everyday."

....

Day 107: Twilight Tuesday

Challenges are inevitable. They are as surefire as night and day. The question is, will you be prepared for them?

I won't allow you to quit, run away, or surrender your belief in yourself. Let's not be naïve. We must acknowledge that there will be hard times. We must prepare for them and build strong character, so we can persevere.

Darkness may be emerging. It may be a challenging time in your life. However, you always inevitably grow from it. How will you prepare? Preparation will be incredibly helpful for you.

....

Day 108: Wisdom Wednesday

Confucius said, "By three methods we may learn wisdom: First, by reflection, which is noblest; Second, by imitation, which is easiest; and third by experience, which is the bitterest."

I like to leverage all three methods to really stack the deck in my favor. Today, begin to accelerate your path to wisdom by applying all three as well.

Day 109: Thankfulness Thursday

I once read in *The Charisma Myth* by Olivia Fox Cabane that human beings are instinctively wired for "hedonic adaptation," meaning we tend to take our blessings for granted. Simply telling yourself that you should be grateful only makes matters worse, because you will become resentful or guilty for feeling that way.

If you are feeling annoyed or bothered by something today, I want you to sweep through your body and focus on three things you can be grateful for. Maybe it's your sight, or your hearing. Maybe, it's your heart pumping blood into your veins

The blessings I just mentioned are always available to most of us. I must admit that it feels great to take a few moments and bring awareness into and appreciation for these gifts.

Please take my suggestion as an expression of my appreciation for you and life itself.

Day 110: Flame Friday

I have a question for you!

How can you burn so bright and catch fire so all eyes are drawn to you? How can you become so warm that people want to be surrounded you.

You can become irresistible—a linchpin!

"Become so good they can't ignore you."
– Steve Martin

Day 111: Skyrocket Saturday

Greg O'Gallahger says, "To skyrocket your success process, stop delaying, waiting, making excuses and looking to the future."

Act now!

Action always happens in the moment. That moment can occur right now for you. So what are you waiting for? Leap into the life you want for yourself, start building and get to work today!

Day 112: Summit Sunday

No matter what mountain you're climbing right now, remember to enjoy the journey as you move towards the summit. Always plan for what comes next.

When you reach your peak, know that you're just peaking. Once you go as far as you think you can, the real climb begins.

As Zig Ziglar says, "See you at the top."

Day 113: Mountain Monday

As I climbed to the top of a mountain with some friends, I realized something.

When I was at the bottom, all I could see were other mountains directly above and in front of me. However, as I neared the summit, I could see out for hundreds of miles, in every direction!

In many ways life is just like that. When we are down and struggling, we tend to only focus on our immediate problems—the enormous mountains ahead. However, once we rise up, the sight of endless possibilities comes into view.

Perspectives are powerful! Goals I didn't believe were possible are now attainable to me because I elevated my game and I can see them now.

· ·

Day 114: Trail Tuesday

I once intentionally veered off the trail while I was hiking and found an epic area.

I find this lesson to be equally as pertinent in life as well. If you do what your family and friends want you to do, you miss your own authentic expression.

Therefore, "Do not go where the path may lead, go instead where there is no path and leave a trail."
- Ralph Waldo Emerson

Find your own lane.

....

Day 115: Wisdom Wednesday

Are you creating and walking the bridge to your dreams?

Taking actions that you know will serve you, will bridge the gap between your current state and your goal for the future.

Jim Rohn says, "Discipline is the bridge between goals and accomplishments."

....

Day 116: Thankfulness Thursday

I'm super grateful for my buddy Mark Dhamma, who once invited me out to Los Angles and offered me some amazing opportunities.

Who are you grateful for?

....

Day 117: Fog Friday

Avoid brain fog. Get rest to recharge. Eat food that serves you. Read, practice gratitude, exercise and be aware of what is most important in your life.

On a macro level, avoid life fog.

"Most of us live in a fog. It's like life is a movie we arrived to

20 minutes late. You know something important seems to be going on. But we can't figure out the story. We don't know what part we're supposed to play or what the plot is." – John Eldredge

Reclaim your will, agenda, and purpose today. Slice through the fog of unconsciousness. Rise above it. Wake up, my friend!

••

Day 118: Skull Saturday

Mark Dhamma says most people put their money outside their skulls with lipstick, haircuts, earrings, etc. It's vital that you invest in the inside your head! Double down on your own brain.

He mentions three great ways in which we can do that:

1. Nutrition
2. Education
3. Meditation

••

Day 119: Shield Sunday

In the story, Pilgrim's Progress, a warrior owns a magical shield.

This shield made him fully invincible—under one condition— he had to face his problems head on with the shield in front of him.

If he got scared and started to turn away from his challenges, he suddenly became vulnerable.

So are you avoiding anything in your path? How might that make you vulnerable?

Pick up your shield and move directly towards your fears!

Day 120: Mantra Monday

Mantra means a tool for thought.

So what is your mantra?

Certain elephants in India are allowed to go into the market place. However, they are given something to put in their mouth, which discourages them from grabbing everything with their trunks. It keeps them disciplined. Your mantra can do the same for you—limiting the commotion in your life.

In order to avoid falling off track, getting distracted, and pulling away from your goals you need a grounding tool. What is one word that will ground you and keep you on track for manifesting your vision?

Maybe it's *focus* or *intensity* or *blessed* or *action*. You decide.

Day 121: Trust-Fund-Baby Tuesday

I was not born into a wealthy family with a sweet trust fund waiting for me.

However, I was blessed to learn that if I show up daily, work hard and serve others with virtue, I would be rewarded richly.

Imagine that you have infinite amount of money waiting for you when you hit a certain age. However there is a caveat, you can only access it when you work for it playfully, persistently, passionately, and patiently. We all already have that trust fund.

It feels incredible to recognize that I have an epic little trust fund and an equally reliable way to access it. This can be a terrific mind trick to tap into that .

tenacity in tough times

⋯⋯⋯⋯⋯⋯⋯⋯⋯⋯⋯⋯⋯⋯⋯⋯⋯⋯⋯⋯⋯⋯⋯⋯⋯⋯⋯⋯⋯⋯⋯⋯⋯⋯⋯⋯⋯⋯⋯

Day 122: Wisdom Wednesday

It doesn't matter how hard and fast you go if you're on the wrong path.

Are you on the path you decided?

Are you moving towards the destination of your choice?

> The greatest thing in the world is not where we are, but which direction we are moving. As Jim Rohn says, "We can't change our destination over night, but you can change our direction."

Seek advice. Become introspective. Don't spend your resources trying to get somewhere you don't want be.

Day 123: Thankfulness Thursday

Last year I went to an event that altered the course of my life! The investment was a big risk, but as a result, I made some high quality relationships, learned a ton, and had epic experiences.

Today, I am eager to do it all again. I'm inspired to infuse my passion, increase my financial skills, and learn ways to help you.

I have leveled up. How can you level up today?

....

Day 124: Face Your Fears Friday

You have to get out of your comfort zone everyday. Today, do something that scares you. Lay on the floor in a public place for ten seconds. Sing in the middle of Starbucks. Wear something embarrassing in front of other people.

Be comfortable being uncomfortable.

....

Day 125: Stab Saturday

It's easy to learn new things, but sometimes it can be hard to maintain them.

I'm blessed to be absorbing astonishing ideas and igniting incredible inspiration inside me. I'm in awe of the inspiration that burns inside the people around me.

When we fail to take action, this inspiration withers away. Our minds create excuses and rationalizations.

I challenge all who are inspired to increase your momentum through excited experimentation and testing.

You can fill your cup with knowledge and inspiration, but all it takes a couple stabs in the sides or the bottom, and everything will spill out. Those stabs are your limiting beliefs. Avoid them and your cup will remain full.

Day 126: Speed of Implementation Sunday

Tell your brain you will do something, and you will trick your brain into believing you have already done it.

It's an astounding fact of neuroscience that emotional satisfaction can occur before you even act. This concept is known as moral satiety. Essentially, by saying you will do something, you experience the benefits of actually doing it. After you have already been emotional rewarded, the urge to actually do it fades.

Act now! Do it with speed. It's what you need… or one can be late, break their word and not finish in Excellence. What that does is use more time and will power overall!

Day 127: Mobilize Monday

You can connect people very naturally when you move forward with passion and purpose. When you are deeply dedicated to the process, amazing things happen.

My friend, Neil Orkin, supported me richly on my journey. I returned the favor. Now, he uses alliteration, stimulating environments, and unique insight to create powerful videos everyday. When your soul burns bright and that flame spreads onto another individual, then they can burn just as brightly as you or hopefully even brighter!

> "We can't help everybody but everybody can help someone." – Ronald Regan

Bring others along, get inspired, and get empowered. Don't do things merely by yourself. You are riding a rollercoaster, but you are never alone. There is always someone by your side. Woooo!

Day 128: Treasure Tuesday

Reading is an incredible habit that leads to success. My top 3 books have been

1. Awaken The Giant Within-Tony Robbins
2. Power of Now-Eckhart Tolle
3. The Way of The Peaceful Warrior-Dan Millman

What are yours? And what was the gold from it that made it so impactful?

> Walt Disney said, "There is more treasure in books, than in all the pirates' loot on Treasure Island."

Leaders are readers.

....

Day 129: Wisdom Wednesday

Does your brain establish links, connections and relationships to resourceful knowledge?

My message today, is to challenge yourself to expand your neural net as well.

Your brain is a SPONGE, full of connections, and the key is to constantly expand those connections—growing them wider and deeper.

How do you do that? Through books, events, seminars, friends, your circle of influence. Keep feeding your brain and strengthening your neural net.

....

Day 130: Testing Thursday

Back to back at the track with a good friend Matt Gallant.

Track yourself to stay on track. Test yourself to be your best. If you are not testing, you're guessing. You will end up lacking and slacking if you are not tracking.

If you are not testing and tracking, you are leaving a fortune on the table. Often the best way to increase your profits is to keep testing your rate of success.

Test!

....

Day 131: Furious Friday

Look for the lessons in hardships.

Ask, what is the world teaching me? Why will I be thankful later on in life for my current situation? Try to get curious instead of furious. Get fascinated instead of frustrated!

If you implement this, you can experience a powerful shift! A lovely leadershift!

Sometimes you get tripped up in life. When it happens, don't sweat it. Become curious to objectively discover what happened. Turn frustration into fascination.

....

Day 132: Sand Saturday

You are like one grain of sand in a beach full of it. There are billions of people in this world.

However, never place your happiness in someone else. Refuse to settle. Live in alignment with your values and truth.

Be free, fun, open, honest abundant and purposeful while you walk your own path.

Come from the whole of you and not the hole in you.

So be purposeful and driven on your mission. Find your vision and your truth.

....

Day 133: Shovel Sunday

Beware of shiny object syndrome. In the movie Holes, the inmates would repeatedly dig wholes five feet deep. Instead of following that pattern, Stanley and Zero dug deep and wide while digging in one spot, and they found riches.

Focus is power. Concentration is critical! Dedication will give you elevation. Use your wits and commit.

If you dig too many shallow holes, you will miss the treasure.

....

Day 134: Muscle Monday

I invite you to see this empowering perspective. It supported me in difficult times. You are a muscle fiber. When you are torn, you will only grow back more powerful.

Your response when you are down determines how fast you'll get back up.

Be resilient. Bounce don't break, baby!

> "If you want resurrection, you must have crucifixion."
> – Joseph Campbell

Day 135: Traffic Tuesday

Most people let traffic bother them. However, you could enjoy the view, listen to a podcast or audiobook, or call your family for a meaningful conversation.

Practice turning perceived negatives into something positive. Practice doing the opposite of what you think you should do.

Day 136: Wisdom Wednesday

Embrace the acronym C.A.N.I. (Constant and Never Ending Improvement)

Whether I become a billionaire at age 64, or at hit rock bottom again—becoming a bum in the slums—I will still love the process of learning and progress.

Once I took ownership and responsibility and decided to dedicate myself to improvement, my life started to improve.

Have you made that bold resolution yet?

Beware challenges will arise with that standard of living, however, many marvelous rich rewards will come as well— including the fulfillment you experience from giving and being your best.

Day 137: Thankfulness Thursday

I used to be afraid of dogs. A dog bit me when I was younger. Now we get along, because I moved towards the thing that scared me. I lived with a big German shepherd during my senior year of college.

As Emerson said, "Do the thing you fear, and the death of fear is certain." I'm grateful for that experience, because as I move forward, I will continue to face F.E.A.R. (False Evidence Appearing Real)

What is one frightening challenge that you can overcome by facing it? Expose yourself to it. It's the fastest band-aid ripped off way to experience freedom.

Day 138: Fork Friday

Oftentimes we make life more difficult than it has to be.

Why dig a hole with your hands when you can use a shovel or an excavator?

Why start a business by yourself when you could create a team or tap into resources on the Internet? The list goes on!

Choose specific and resourceful tools that will help you accomplish your goals.

Day 139: Shanti Saturday

Shanti means peace in Hindi. Today, my friends and I encourage you guys do whatever brings peace into your life—whether that is meditation, walking, or listening to your favorite song. Whatever you choose spread the peace.

I am blessed to have such great souls around me.

Together we share our peace with you. We wish that you enjoy the sacred moments of life.

Find ways to access calm, contentment, confidence, and trust. Find these feelings in activities that serve you.

Namaste.

Day 140: Serendipity Sunday

It is such a blessing to be a part of this world—a world where everything is connected and challenges happen for a reason.

Keep believing and trusting that life will unfold in the perfect order, even if you cannot see it now.

Life is serendipitous. When you fall short of your goal, it could be a blessing in disguise. You might receive something far greater than you ever imagined. Be open to that.

Day 141: Mineral Spring Monday

I went to a spa recently, and it was euphoric.

It was the most rejuvenating experience I have had in my life. However, rejuvenation doesn't have to be that fancy.

How are you unwinding after grinding?

Remember to recover, recharge, replenish, and revive after a long hard day.

Day 142: Top Speed Tuesday

Is there something lying around that you have not finished?

Identify something that you have been putting off and go all out on it. Crank it up to top speed on. Bang it out today, and finish strong.

Day 143: Wisdom Wednesday

I challenge you to think back to a time that you made a wish. Now, write it down as a goal. Seek and share it with someone you trust and who can support you.

Create a strategy to bring it about, and absolutely take action on it.

Lastly, plan your celebration and reward when you attain it. Enjoy the manifestation that comes with the process!

Day 144: Thankfulness Thursday

Sometimes society forces us to be average. It tells us our potential is limited.

This message makes me want to sharpen up in various areas of my life. I seek to understand how to avoid societal groupthink and where to redirect my focus.

When you do this, you will discover what you can accomplish. You will begin to see how much is possible. Don't get forced into societal belief systems—or as I like to call them BS. Learn what actions, foods, and resources will serve you.

I am so grateful to be writing my own ticket in life—to be the boss of my own brain. Can you identify a limit that has been placed on you by others?

Appreciate the Awareness

Day 145: Ferry Friday

When you have a positive or negative experience, know you are not alone! Knowing that others are sharing your experiences can provide immense peace when you are feeling down.

You won't feel odd, strange, or abnormal. You can stop judging yourself, and open up avenues for compassion and love.

Knowing there are other people in the same boat helps you get out of your head.

....

Day 146: Shoot Saturday

Before you take action, you may feel stifled and nervous. Just like arrow about to be fired away, you experience tension before you shoot towards your target. That tension and tightness absolutely, scientifically will go away the more you take action. You will get used to it, and the fear will fade.

Remember to let go of the result of your actions. Learn from them, but don't seek validation from other people. Relax and do your best. Then adjust from feedback, and take action again.

....

Day 147: Squash Sunday

Today, I offer you a reminder to take full ownership of the outstanding opportunities awaiting you.

Bust them open—instead of hoping!

What opportunities, goals, and fears can you absolutely smash?

....

Day 148: Meritorious Monday

What can you pat yourself on the back for accomplishing? Acknowledge what you have done.

My military friend @saaiman_says, "The definition of meritorious is admirable and praiseworthy."

What have you done for yourself, your family, or your friends that is admirable and praiseworthy? Take an action today that you can be proud of tomorrow.

....

Day 149: Ta-Tuesday

I once hosted a seminar at the Muscle Mansion and was able to connect some awesome individuals.

One thing I learned was the sound of "Ta" opens the heart. Ta is the spiritual Mantra for the heart. Try speaking that mantra today.

How does it make you feel?

Maybe explore other sounds and notice their gifts.

....

Day 150: Wisdom Wednesday

I always seek to set myself up to win.

In the past, I have hopped on a flight with only a enough money for food. I decided to find a place to live when I arrived. After I commit and am completely invested in something, my "shoulds," become "musts." I find a way to make things work because I have to.

It's a resourceful strategy to use once in awhile when action is lacking. If its a worthy opportunity then jump in and figure out the how later!

How will you apply the principle of burning the boats?

. . . .

Day 151: Thankfulness Thursday

Spent some time in L.A. recently. It rarely rains there, but it did while I was visiting. So I soaked it up. It feels great to let the rain hit your skin—especially when you don't get rain often. We don't know what we have until it's gone. Rain can bring us down, but we cannot live without it.

Take notice of what you can show gratitude for something right now in your life while it is there.

. . . .

Day 152: Fortune Friday

Fortune isn't something that you find. It's something that unfolds as you create it.

Make your own luck. Believe in your fortune right now.

. . . .

Day 153: Self Saturday

Many people will hate you. Many people will like you. Regardless of other opinions, do you.

"Be who you are and say what you feel because those who mind don't matter and those who matter don't mind." – Dr. Seuss

There are billions of people on the planet. Not everyone will like you. Not everyone will hate you. But some people will follow you to the ends of the earth. Those are your people. Find them.

....

Day 154: Strength Camp Sunday

In my mentor Elliott Hulse's business, Strength Camp, the core values are accountability, coaching, programing, and most importantly, community.

Each are critical to it's success and impact

Take this time to reflect on your top four virtuous characteristics of paramount importance.

....

Day 155: Mindset Monday

My friend Brandon Carter brings raw intensity to his goals. He now has an accomplished YouTube channel and successful fitness business. He advises not to follow your dreams but to hunt them!

Are you accessing that ruthlessness, relentless hunger to drive you towards your dreams?

As Brandon Carter says, "Always remember, that which gets measured–gets managed."

Record, strategize, and reflect. Remember, if you are not testing you're guessing.

Day 156: Testosterone Tuesday

Why do native Indians have so many babies? Because they eat amazing, healthy, testosterone-boosting food. Resistance training and great sleep can boost your Testosterone.

Testosterone leads to an incredible sex drive and increased energy. There are many other health advantages you can reap by eating certain foods, getting adequate rest and physical activity.

To learn more about testosterone, follow my friend @ doctortestorone on instagram.

Day 157: Wisdom Wednesday

Boxer, bodybuilder, and YouTuber, Mike Rashid, once gave me some great advice that I want to share with you today.

Put yourself in challenging situations. Give them your all, and grow from them. If you fail to challenge yourself, you'll have to acknowledge that you left something on the table— you didn't pour your heart out. As a result, you will never be satisfied.

Day 158: Thanksgiving Thursday

This is probably one of my favorite quotes:

"Wherever you are, be there." – Jim Rohn

It's a simple reminder to enjoy, embrace, accept, acknowledge, and appreciate the here and now.

Gratitude is a standard of living for me. I know that if we can overcome the barriers of expectation and accept the now, we can see the blessings all around us. Give up comparisons and immerse yourself in the moment while you enjoy your evolution.

....

Day 159: Ferrari Friday

Create a great engine. Cleanse your body with wholesome foods. Recharge with proper rest. Condition with top-notch exercise. Seek high quality as often as you can.

If you are treating your pet, car, or house better than yourself, please take a moment to think about that.

Zoom fast and fix that! Create the engine of a Ferrari to power your progress.

....

Day 160: Shoe Saturday

I enjoy crossing paths with people along this unique journey of life. I become fascinated with the way that they view the world.

By seeing the world through their lens, not only do I learn a lot, but I can also help people to feel understood.

Start walking in other people's shoes, and see life through their eyes. You will find a much more effective approach for your relationships. Seeking first to understand, then to be understood. Find their unique motivations and offer value that way.

Day 161: Savor Sunday

I practice mindful eating a few times a week and it always, tremendously enhances my eating experience. No videos or distractions just what's in front of me.

By taking the time to honor the food and the miraculous process that went into creating it, I can truly appreciate its magic. There are months of planting, growing, gathering, transporting, and cooking behind every food you eat.

Take extra time to enjoy your food by using all your senses, smell, touch, and taste. Chew slowly, and bless the food for where it came from and all the work that went into creating it.

Day 162: Mime Monday

It's lovely how creative and captivating a mime can be with merely movement. More than half of communication is body language, so devote attention to making yours more effective. Additionally, by altering your posture and patterns

of movement, you can make yourself feel great. Emotion is motion!

Mimes are all epic copycats. Muster up the ability and the memory to mimic those who are at the top. Study specialists and model your behaviors after them.

Soon you will experience similar results. Progress from imitation to emulation to mutation—eventually creating your own remixed style.

<hr />

Day 163: Tiptoe Tuesday

Too many people take half-hearted actions. When you face a challenge fully, you can commit and follow it through to completion. Many great teachers have shared the philosophy that focus is essential for success.

When you jump into freezing cold water it will be shocking. However, once you splash around a bit, you will begin to feel exhilarated.

Wholehearted actions work in the same way. Jump into something wholeheartedly today.

<hr />

Day 164: Wisdom Wednesday

Get out of your own way!

We are often our own biggest blockades. Realize how you might be holding yourself back, and then adjust accordingly.

In the movie Creed, Rocky says, "The person in the mirror is the toughest opponent you are going to face."

How can you get out of your own way today?

....

Day 165: Thankfulness Thursday

I could do a thankfulness entry everyday.

I'm so grateful for the big sun in the sky—shining on me—giving me that vitamin D. Appreciate the breeze and the smell of the seasonal air.

What in nature can you appreciate and be grateful for?

....

Day 166: Face Friday

We all wear masks to create a façade. These masks keep us in the prison of perfection, forged by the opinion of others.

Instead, create a game face. Wear that face everyday. Tell your face now!!

> "What we face may look insurmountable. But I learned something from all those years of training and competing. I learned something from all those sets and reps when I didn't think I could lift another ounce of weight. What I learned is that we are always stronger than we know." – Arnold Schwarzenegger

Day 167: Stairs Saturday

It's been said there isn't an elevator or escalator to success. You must take the stairs. You are going to have to work. Whenever there is a choice, take the stairs. Let it remind your brain that to get to the top, you must put in work.

The best work you can put in is the work you put into yourself!

As Jim Rohn said, "Work on yourself harder than you do on your job."

Don't accept the reality you've been given. Create your own life.

"We should not look back unless it is to derive useful lessons from past errors." – George Washington

Gain wisdom from the past and learn from yourself and others. Let go of guilt, judgment, regret and feel free until you to scream out load and rejoice.

••

Day 168: Service Sunday

The secret to living is giving.

A team and I once planted one hundred and fifteen trees at a retreat and it felt incredible.

Enjoy the generosity you give and make it extraordinary.

Give with one hand, and you will receive with the other.

Day 169: Move of Power Monday

I always get tremendous positive feedback on my energy. I believe it's because I do subtle simple power moves throughout my day. Emotion is motion.

You have the power to change how you feel by using your body. Feel empowered, elated, and excited through deliberate physical action today.

Think of a time you felt your very best! Get specific on that time. Once you got it activate all senses! Then make it bigger and brighter multiply the feelings times 10 and make a move! do this 10 times and you got your power move you can access anytime!!

Day 170: Twin Tuesday

I know two brothers Eric and Chris Martinez @ dynamicduotraining that support each other and hold each other to a standard of excellence everyday.

I consciously choose to put people in my life who hold me to a higher standard—who won't let me fail.

Who are the top ten friends by your side?

Find a *twin* who will support you even when you are down.

Day 171: Wisdom Wednesday

Most people's minds are so full of conclusions that there is no room for expansion. So what conclusions have you made that you may need to challenge?

Don't become deeply attached to all of your ideas or beliefs. Eventually, new ideas might arise that will serve you more fully from the new situation you are in. When you let go, you create room to grow!

"The mind is like a parachute it only works if it's open." – Oscar Wilde

Day 172: Thankfulness Thursday

To trick your mind into appreciating something more fully, imagine if it were taken away.

Now imagine having it back again.

Sometimes it takes loss to make us realize what we have.

Day 173: Faithful Friday

Almost all major religions share these two philosophies: See the unseen and faith without action, is death. So couple faith with action today!

"Faith is taking the first step even when you don't see the whole staircase." – Martin Luther King, Jr.

"Faith is the bird that feels the light when the dawn is still dark." – Tagore

"The attitude of faith is the very opposite of clinging to belief, of holding on." –Alan Watts

....

Day 174: Spectacle Saturday

Great art is often a spark of Divine creation. My cousin, Joseph Young, created a triforium in downtown Los Angeles forty years ago. It still amazes many today.

How are you expressing the sacred creativity residing within you so it can stand the test of time?

....

Day 175: Shortcut Sunday

Avoid the shortcuts in life and take the smart cuts.

Smart cuts are strategies to help you grow. They may not be easier now, but in the long run they will make things easier. Accelerate your progress by hitting your pinnacle of potential with these smart cuts:

1. Accountability
2. Mentors

3. Failing forward fast
4. Being generous
5. Time for self-care
6. Embarking on the hero's journey (the insecure way is the secure way!)

Day 176: Major Monday

What if you were to focus on the sounds around you right now, instead of the text on this page?

See how we can shift our focus. What if you were see the specks on the window rather than the sunset?

What about being right rather than the result...

How about your family members hair over their heart.

Small things are important, but they aren't as important as big things.

Too many of us major in the minor things of life. The main thing is to keep the main, the main thing. Still nail the detail but never forget the big picture!

Day 177: Time Tuesday

You can create your reality by having empowering beliefs. Proactively pick what you wish to live for. Avoid adopting the societal BS (belief systems) that was pushed on you. It is your time! but for you to own it you must be you and do you!

> "We are defined by the stories we tell ourselves."
> – Tony Robbins

> "Time is a created thing." – Lao Tzu

> "We must use time wisely and forever realize that the time is always ripe to do right." – Nelson Mandela

Day 178: Wisdom Wednesday

> President Andrew Jackson once said, "One man with courage makes a majority."

It's easy to follow the crowd and be complacent, but the majority of civilization has unfortunately learned helplessness.

How can you implement the principle of inversion where you reverse engineer your long term goal to today to revolutionize your life and differentiate yourself from your future competitors?!?!

Day 179: Thankfulness Thursday

I still train insane, however, not as intensely as I used to when I wrestled. The training was tough, but it made me tougher.

"Once you wrestled, everything else in life is easy"
– Dan Gable

I am grateful for the character I built by training with such purpose.

I am appreciative I pushed past my limits. Now I can appreciate basketball, lifting, and swimming.

Have you trained super hard for a goal? Do you appreciate the freedom and skill you earned through that demanding training?

Appreciate the contrast that comes with progress.

....

Day 180: Forgiveness Friday

Conflicts and grudges can lock you into a mental prison.

"To forgive is to set a prisoner free and discover that the prisoner was you." – Lewis B. Smedes

"The weak can never forgive. Forgiveness is the attribute of the strong." – Gandhi

Understanding that everyone is trying their best will improve your relationships and open you up to the beautiful world around you. See other people in their greatness.

Day 181: Surf Saturday

Don't ask if challenges will come, ask when they will come? Because they will!!

How will you be able to handle them?

As life progresses we gain more wisdom. With this wisdom we will grow stronger.

> The Peaceful Warrior, Dan Millman, says, "Life comes to us in waves. We can't control or predict those waves in life, but we can learn to surf."

So how are you overcoming your challenges, going with the flow, and rising above your obstacles?

Day 182: Seashore Sunday

Some things in life will come easy. However, the most fulfilling accomplishments are the ones earned with courage, discipline, and character.

Create attraction with action. Be a magnet by being ecstatic and by applying successful habits.

> A Chinese proverb says, "Pearls don't fly on the seashore, if you want one, you have to dive in and get it."

Go grab and retrieve the great shiny gems of opportunities awaiting you! Do it joyfully and urgently as if you are sprinting into the ocean diving into it for the first time!

Day 183: Make Decisions Monday

Decision comes from the root word incision, which means to "cut off."

So when you decide, you must cut off all other possibilities. It will make you more focused, effective, aggressive, and successful!

Eliminate half-hearted approaches to what you want. Eradicate excuses and get in the flow of doing.

Day 184: Transfer Tuesday

You won't always be in an environment that supports you and your vision. When you are challenged by your environment, you have three options:

1. Accept it
2. Remove/replace it
3. Find more empowering meanings for it

I once safely moved a baby bumblebee away from my workout space so I wouldn't get stung. How can you do something similar in your life?

Day 185: Wisdom Wednesday

To save massive amounts of time and energy, create an inner locus of control. Take responsibility for every aspect of your life and don't complain. Power is found within you, not in the external world. Get more creative, resourceful, compassionate, and committed to creating your dream life.

Day 186: Thankfulness Thursday

I am so grateful to have grown up in Norristown, PA with my family. The experiences I have had and the people that I have met have made me the person I am today.

Are you grateful for your hometown? What in it can you be grateful for?

And if you moved around awesome even more gratitude for you!!

Day 187: Five Friday

You are the average of the five people you hang around the most. Look around you. Are you okay with being around those types of people?

We absorb everything from the foods we eat, to our friends, to our music. Control your environment or your environment will control you.

Day 188: Skate Saturday

The first time I went ice-skating was very fun and inspiring.

When you are on thin ice in life, that's when you will bring your best. Whenever I'm in precarious situations, I am more alive and motivated. I perform better with my back against the wall.

How can you get you out of your comfort zone and into a sticky situation, so you are compelled to bring your best? Or if you are not in one now can you imagine you are so you play BIGGER?!

Day 189: Seal Sunday

For many people, Sunday is a day to rest and recover, but not for us.

If you are getting after it like me—having a blast on the journey—then today is a great day to turn off the television. Hit the gym, eat healthy, connect deeply to those closest to you and work on your top priorities with sense of urgency.

Don't be a lazy seal lying on the beach. Today, be a shark and hunt for what you want.

Day 190: Mistake Monday

My good friend Julian says, "Losers are repeaters. Not only are they repeating their own mistakes, but they are also repeating the mistakes of their family and their culture. Winners have the courage to take what they learn. Make changes and make a difference."

Make a difference today!

....

Day 191: Too Tuesday

I will go to the extreme to create the results I want.

However, don't do *too* much.

Broccoli is incredibly healthy, but *too* much will make you sick. Partying can be fun, but party every night, and you will pay the price. Avoid losing your balance by leaning *too* far in one direction

When you feel like you are trying too hard, that is a sign of too much resistance with your current approach. There is probably a better way to accomplish your goal, so pivot and switch it up. Be *too* blessed to be stressed, and remember to do things in moderation.

....

Day 192: Wisdom Wednesday

Ricky Vitucci, the executive assistant of a successful marijuana company, revealed that to become successful he did these three things:

1. Leaped into the unknown
2. Stuck to his beliefs while keeping an open mind
3. Expected to be victorious

Ricky said, "Screw it, I am moving to LA. I moved here without knowing anybody and that was the best decision I ever made. So, don't ever give up, always strive and always do what you believe in and success will come."

Day 193: Thankfulness Thursday

Life is tough but I'm determined to be tougher. My belief in my tenacity has always supported me.

I am grateful that when I faced the most difficult obstacle in my life, I didn't quit. Instead, I recommitted to my success in much a deeper and more impactful way.

Reflect for a moment.

What are you most appreciative of in your yearly performance?

Day 194: Fact Friday

You can reverse engineer the process of creating a fact. Believe that you can create whatever you want, and it will become a fact.

Right now, life might not be what you want it to be. However, the fact is you can change that.

Change your perspectives, ideas, virtues, and beliefs and you will change your life.

"We cannot change our past. We cannot change the fact that people act in a certain way. We cannot change the inevitable. The only thing we can do is play on the one string we have, and that is our attitude."
– Charles R. Swindoll

Day 195: Survival Saturday

Even when it's coldest outside, you can always look within to find a fierce fire that will keep you warm.

Surviving a winter, literally or figuratively, is about looking deep inside your heart and discovering the flames that will help you thrive.

The next time you feel resistance send acceptance and unconditional love in that direction.

Day 196: Samurai Sunday

When a samurai takes a step in different direction, he sees the world through another perspective. So every step you take, stop and course correct.

With each change of direction and new perspectives, evaluate the situation. Take notice of life from different angles.

This will not only keep you from falling off track, but also will help you become laser focused on your goals.

Correct course, stay on track, and be like the samurai!

Day 197: Model Monday

So many people want to be models, but not many people want to be role models.

Today, model people who are successful in the fields that you specialize in.

As a leader, be an example for others on your path. People may copy you, but that's because they respect and admire you.

Who are you emulating currently? How can you help others emulate you?

Day 198: Tall Tuesday!

Walking down Hollywood Boulevard u see a statue of Robert Wadlow—the tallest man to ever live. He was 8'11".

Reminded me of the question and idea of how tall will a tree grow? As tall as it is genetically programed to grow. However, human potential is different. Your potential for success isn't predetermined. It is something that you can choose. Your mindset, skills, achievements will power your potential for success.

I am personally committed to self-actuality—to reach my full potential.

What is your personal commitment to growth?

....

Day 199: Wisdom Wednesday

Was blessed to have a roommate that had well over 50 million dollar a year company was super successful and genuine guy named Big Mike. @Bigmike is convicted that we absolutely must believe in ourselves. He believes we are the products of our beliefs.

Become responsible for your mindset and discard the trash.

The three ways he suggests to do that are:

1. Read and have a library

2. Surround yourself with great people and mastermind

3. Speak your truth because the most vulnerable one gets the most respect

"But first you have to believe in yourself. You have to. You are your own product, so you have to believe in making you. There is a lot of head trash that we all carry around and you got to get rid of it." – Big Mike

....

Day 200: Thankfulness Thursday

I am grateful that my brain recognizes patterns. You have the gift of pattern recognition, as well.

The more people do something, the more they improve. Once you take action, you notice certain subtle ways that become much more effective and aggressive in what you do.

Trust that your subconscious mind will figure things out along the way. Take strategic action while focusing on learning. You will reap amazing results and have an awesome journey. Take a breath and exhale.

Day 201: Fundamental Friday

"Success isn't magical or mysterious. It is the natural consequence of consistently applying the basic fundamentals." – Jim Rohn

Handle the basics and practice them consistently. Living in a 30,000$ a month mansion and seeing how high performers work I found that to be true. Along with traveling the United States, I learned from some of the happiest, richest, kindest, smartest, and most influential people. They all believe fundamental habits are essential and there is for sure enough data to back that up.

A giant limiter for me was I had tons of wild and preposterous black and white/this or that stories in my mind that like rich people have special talents and inherit the money or step on others to get to the top and lack the ability for fun. The list goes on, however after massive exposure I saw these tricks in my mind for what they were excuses for me not to work.

Once one can get that almost any outcomes are achievable and possible without the rationalizations ask:

What fundamentals of living a great life do I feel are important? Am I making a habit of practicing them regularly?

Day 202: Staircase Saturday

Nothing is a waste of time. Use every life experience—good or bad—as a stepping-stone to your goal. Transmute your past and present into gold, like an alchemist!

In an interview, Johnny Depp said that his first acting gig was his job as a telemarketer. He used every experience of his life to actualize his greatest self.

Become great and climb the staircase of success and imagine those are golden stairs with lessons and blessings at each step.

Day 203: Spread the Love Sunday

Love is the greatest gift you can give as a spiritual being.

So don't hold back the opportunity to give the wealthiest gift you have—whether or not you feel like it. Give it and then you will feel like it! It could be a smile, hug, kind words or all the above!

Stay great and always give love.

Day 204: Many Monday

Creators don't have much time to consume and spectate—let alone be envious.

Remember, you are creative. So if you are not sharing your gift, you are doing a disservice to yourself and the world. There are people waiting to benefit from your courageous contributive actions. Do and be something of value. Create and make something of service.

See the few who do are the envy of the many that watch.

Limit consumption and increase creation! Stop hating or spectating and start participating.

Day 205: Tongue Twister Tuesday

Tongue Twister Tuesday! Say this swiftly, sweetly, and sharply.

Say this strongly, smartly, and shortly.
Shoot, say this sensationally.
Shit, say it stupendously.

Say this in succession sixteen times:

"I will take massive action to cause attraction and passion!"

> I like repeating things again and again to drive the point home. As Jim Rohn says, "Affirmation without discipline is the beginning of delusion."

Affirmations coupled with action makes one feel unstoppable.

....

Day 206: Wisdom Wednesday

I've always strived to be different, which can be both helpful and hurtful. However, when reaching out to your ideal advisor or mentor, you should strive to be different and stand out in a positive way.

That goes for anything. Always go above and beyond. Offer twelve times what is expected.

What are you doing that is out of the norm? Get creative to get the results you desire.

Be different! Remember, some resumes stand out, others get lost amongst the rest.

....

Day 207: Thankfulness Thursday

A surefire way to become a super positive person is to identify and experience appreciation for the gifts that you have been given. What are you grateful for?

Today, let's test it.

Start with a little notebook. Identify five different things that you appreciate and see how they make you feel as you appreciate them. Do it again tomorrow and the next day, and watch the abundance overflow.

Beware! It may attract amazing things into your life. Peace and blessings.

....

Day 208: Fine Art Friday

"The earth without art is just 'eh.'" I love that quote.

Seriously, life can be just 'eh' sometimes. It can be plain and lame if we don't create our own design for it. Look at life like your canvas. How will you paint it?

Are you equipped with the tools you need to succeed and can you color it in a way that excites you?

If we can get creative enough we can either use the right tools or discover alternatives that will make something even more spectacular.

But remember, beauty is in the eye of the beholder. Therefore, create it for yourself.

....

Day 209: Shark Saturday

When swimming in the ocean, everyone fears the shark. However, there are many other things that can harm you— strong currents, big waves, other predatory fish.

The most obvious threat isn't always the most immediate or the most dangerous. This law applies to your thoughts as well.

Observe your thoughts for just an hour and notice how many false, foolish, and damaging thoughts pop up. Take notice of how insignificant they are when you bring them into your awareness. Sometimes in social situations we magnify and even imagine scenarios that make us feel unworthy.

Direct your focus on thoughts that will serve you.

Day 210: Snow Sunday

I will be the first to say that I am not perfect and do not always come from the greatest of intentions. Sometimes I want to win and just take care of me selfishly.

However, when I do come from the sentiment of oneness, appreciation, kindness, and presence, it beautifies the situation.

Love, kindness, generosity, and presence cover the foundation of your interactions like snow. It beautifies them.

Are you covering your interactions with that kind of emotion? Are you coming from that kind of place? It is felt and makes almost all the difference because the self shines through and the way off being is what leading

Day 211: Mentor Monday

My buddy, @YayhaBakkar, has noticed something that many people don't realize.

He said, "Remember if you have a mentor, the mentee is just as valuable as the mentor. So the exchange of value goes both ways. Never forget how valuable you are!"

You can help your mentor in a myriad of ways! Provide space for them to speak and energize them with positivity and a fresh perspective. Remind them of old ideas they value but might have forgotten plus much MUCH more!!

Every relationship has an exchange of energies so keep it win win.

Day 212: Truth Tuesday

@JamesSwanwick attests that reading a book a day, can improve your life on multiple levels.

Does that seem like a stretch for you?

Well, then that is even more of reason for you to do it.

Test this truth for twenty-one days if you dare.

Day 213: Wisdom Wednesday

My friend Cole Hatter and I were chatting about the shortness of life. He shared his favorite quote "You only get one life, but if you use it properly it is more than enough."– John C Maxwell

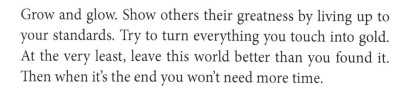

Grow and glow. Show others their greatness by living up to your standards. Try to turn everything you touch into gold. At the very least, leave this world better than you found it. Then when it's the end you won't need more time.

Day 214: Thankfulness Thursday

I am grateful for the dash dance! The dash dance is the journey you take from the moment you are born until the moment you die. It is the hyphen (-) in between your birthdate and death date.

Are you making the most of that journey?

Day 215: Flying Friday

Have you ever had difficulty starting something? Remember, progress is a process. To paraphrase Martin Luther King Jr., just start crawling. Then, start walking. Then, start running. Then, maybe one day, you will fly.

Start with your feet on the ground. Take action with faith, and soon you will soar.

Day 216: Spark Saturday

Visit the places and the people that will ignite a spark in your soul. Then your greatness and your dreams will unfold!

Do you make a wholehearted effort to put yourself around successful, humble, and purposeful people and environment that stimulate you?

Sometimes, I experience resistance. However, I push past it, when I set myself up to win by shifting my space or place which rarely fails to have an impact.

Day 217: Slept Sunday

I am about to share something so beautiful, true, and powerful with you.

> "I have slept and dreamt that life is joy. I awoke realizing that life is service. I acted on it and realized that service is joy." – Tagore

Serve your way to success it is living the dream while awake.

Day 218: Mud Monday

I once did yoga in the mud and got all dirty. Sometimes you have to get down in the mud like a pig and do the grimy work in life. Use this empowering metaphor to encourage you to do the work that no one wants to do.

Is there work that you don't want to do, but know you have to? Do that today and instead say "have to" maybe use want to, or blessed to! This will make a difference. Test it now then play in the mud and feel the buzz of a new perspective.

Day 219: Tantalizing Puzzle Tuesday

Life's answers can seem to be like an array of puzzle pieces more than a key or combination lock.

Therefore, collect them fast, because the sooner you do, the better your life will become. A big part of the puzzle is your education and knowledge.

Find the puzzle pieces and arrange the picture of your dreams.

Day 220: Wisdom Wednesday

"An investment in knowledge always pays the best interest." – Ben Franklin

Get a mentor.

Simple as that.

Day 221: Thankfulness Thursday

It's difficult to suffer from negative emotions when you're in a constant state of gratitude.

Flood yourself with the gratitude and all of your 'problems' will transform into challenges that you can be grateful for. Challenges will put you in the mental, physical, and emotional state to be able to impact as many people as possible.

So every single morning when you wake up, think of three

things you can be grateful for. The fact that you woke up today and have air to breathe is a gift. What is one more?

Day 222: Figure It Out Friday

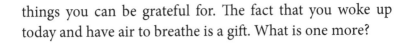

To quote Marie Forleo, "everything is figure-out-able."

Try writing your questions out on paper, look at them everyday. See if the answers will come. It is insane how brilliant our brains are!

Day 223: Solution Saturday

It's epic to see someone come from the bottom and climb up.

Get inspired by everything and everyone. With that mindset, you will really shine.

When I had the pleasure of meeting and interviewing Ralph Smart @infinitewaters, he said, "I am inspired by everything and everyone. Definitely growing up, Fritz Pearls, the psychologist, was big inspiration. So were people like my mom or everyday people!"

How can you do the same?

Day 224: Snippet Sunday

Here is a small snippet of advice and a step from my Millionaire Mentor course:

If you really care about connecting with someone, offer him or her extreme value. They might help you move towards your goals. How can you do the same for them?

Find out what they enjoy. Discover their unique motivations.

Day 225: Motivate the Masses Monday

Everyday we can play big—and do it unapologetically.

During my interview with one of the stars from The Movie The Secret Lisa Nichols says, "Before you check you likes on social media make sure you like yourself first."

"Play big, unapologetically. Make memories by the way you live!" – @Lisa2motivate

Day 226: Trekking Pole Tuesday

Equip yourself with the right tools for the journey.

To climb a magnificent mountain, you have to use tools.

What wild tools are you using to climb towards your dreams and look out on your ideal life?

Day 227: Wisdom Wednesday

"Your attitude, not your aptitude, will determine your altitude." – Zig Ziglar

Be the thermostat rather than the thermometer. Dictate your energy, cheerfulness, and attitude. Control the temperature of your life. Don't let your environment decide everything for you.

......

Day 228: Thankfulness Thursday

People ask me if I ever get negative. I do; however, I try not to stay that way!

Every time you catch yourself being negative, redirect your focus on creating positive energy. Don't allow yourself to stay negative more than three minutes.

If you exchange expectation for appreciation, your life will change forever. Be in a beautiful state, every single day.

......

Day 229: Freaking Amazing Friday

Dean Graziosi suggests:

1. Forget the news.

2. Double down on your strengths and don't dwell on your weaknesses. Delegate your dirty work to others in the most fun way possible.

3. Avoid advice from people who don't have great results in the domain you are seeking advice in.

....

Day 230: Something Saturday

My friend Lisa (@lisa2motivate on instagram) has such a fun, free, and abundant energy. She is a multimillionaire, a speaker, an author, and an entrepreneur. She has even been featured on Oprah.

She says that getting a coach is essential. It leveled her up and continues to.

The absence of a coach will cost you more money in the long run by not having one. It is the something that can change everything!

....

Day 231: Spend Sunday

If you gamble, recognize that you are betting on your outside environment. You are transferring your power to the external world. Instead, bet on yourself because you have control over that.

Write your own ticket in life!

It feels great to have of ownership, autonomy, and self-reliance. Anyone can develop those skills when they bet on themselves.

Day 232: Mission Monday

Vision comes from your head.
Intuition comes from your heart.
Ambition comes from your gut.

What's the mission that has you living driven filled with ambition—in which you are not seeking permission to follow your intuition? I am talking about giving from a virtuous vision. Be ready and willing to make a positive killing.

Day 233: Teacher Tuesday

Teaching is the profession that creates all other professions.

> Henry Adam says, "A teacher affects an eternity; he never can tell where his influence stops."

Let's all teach someone something today!

Day 234: Wisdom Wednesday

Many people ask me to reveal my favorite book.

> To this day, it is the very same book I discovered many years ago, "Awaken The Giant Within." by Tony Robbins. No other book has had more of an impact on me.

Learning how to change, create, and make my own state, story, and strategy gave me a huge edge in life. It taught me about the power of language, good questions, and most of all, modeling success. That book encouraged me to connect with so many mentors. We all have a giant within us. Let's bring it out more frequently.

How can you create your reality and change your destiny?

* * *

Day 235: Thankfulness Thursday

Writing thank you notes is a great weekly habit.

Try writing a handwritten thank you note every Thursday for the next month. Join the revolution—The Thank You Revolution.

* * *

Day 236: Fix Your Mornings Friday

When you wake up tomorrow morning avoid all social media, texts, and email at all costs.

Starting your day off with these distractions puts your brain in reactive mode immediately—a weak recipe for winning.

Set yourself up to win by being at the 'cause' rather than the 'effect' of the day. Be proactive, in charge, and purposeful with your morning routines. Run the day. Don't let the day run you.

A few of my morning rituals include: meditation, dancing, gratitude, and walking.

Day 237: Starving Saturday

Stay hungry for success. Have a big appetite and hunt for your goals.

After Alligators eat they are most vulnerable to be caught or attacked because they over eat, relax and lose most of their power.

Are you full, comfortable, content or cozy, or are you starving and hungry for success in some area?

Day 238: Soul Mate Sunday

I don't believe in soul mates. I believe that everyone is my unique brother or sister. Everyone is special to me in some respect.

If you don't take care of yourself, all your relationships will suffer—romantic, family, or friends. In any relationship, there's always an exchange of energies.

If you lack respect for your health, wealth, happiness, and habits, how do you expect others to respect you? Self-love is the most important love. With self-love, you can offer more and allow yourself to receive more as well.

If you are alone today, remember you are never alone. In fact, break down the word alone and you uncover the truth that you are always "all one" with God—the emanating force of love in the world.

Day 239: Multiply Monday

Want to increase your results in life tenfold? Be more optimistic.

Practice optimism. When you are optimistic, you will become more opportunistic. By focusing on the best results, you will be more passionate and you will optimize your skills and production.

Optimism is a forceful multiplier!

Just focus on being more positive, controlling what you can control, and finding the greatest upside and you will experience exponential results! Balance your high expectations with realism, guidance, strategy, integrity, and momentum and you will become a force to be reckoned with.

Day 240: Treasure Trove Tuesday

One day, the Gods realized that humans were not maximizing their potential, so they decided to hide it from them. One God suggested they put it on top of a mountain, but the other Gods disagreed—expecting humans to simply climb the mountain and retrieve it. Another suggested they put it deep beneath the Earth. However, the other Gods once again disagreed—expecting humans to dig through the Earth and retrieve it. Finally the wisest God spoke. "No let's put their potential deep inside them, so they have to look within to find it."

Are all the answers within? I feel it's both within and out in the world. Yet we neglect within much more.

Make your outer world a reflection of your inner world. However, before you can do that you must know them both.

· ·

Day 241: Wisdom Wednesday

Some people say they are shy well it would be wise not to buy that story they tell themselves.

> "The world suffers alot and not because of the violence of bad people, but because of the silence of good people." – Napoleon Bonaparte

So speak up and shout your authentic voice. Share your message!

· ·

Day 242: Thankfulness Thursday

I am grateful for my clothes—which keep me warm, my bags—which hold my belongings, and my eyes—which see the beauty all around me.

Find gratitude in simplicity, and it will give you an attitude of blissful electricity.

Day 243: Finesse Friday

Focus on subtleties and you will manifest dramatic improvements. Small things can make a huge difference.

So play with poise and improve that small skill.

Day 244: Sideways Saturday

Exploring Laguna Beach California I stumbled across a sideways palm tree and it looked like the roots were about to break from the dirt. It reminded me how ineffective it can be for running backs in football to right to left too much. Instead, in your life Keep moving north and south. Keep going forward.

> You may take a step back from time to time. However, don't dillydally around. "If don't stand for something, you will fall for anything." – Alexander Hamilton

Stand straight and firm for what you believe in.

Day 245: Silence Sunday

Scramble the letters in the word 'silent' and you will discover the word 'listen' within it. Spend, at minimum, twenty minutes a day in silence. Get comfortable with not speaking.

You will soon become more sensitive to your best self, and

you will tap into your incredible intuition. Always notice what thoughts arise when you are sitting in silence.

"Prayer is when you talk to God. Meditation is when God talks to you."

Day 246: Mansion Monday

Explore the new rooms of your mind. Most people are stuck in a room the size of a jail cell. By being open to explore new rooms of our minds, we find a vastness of opportunity.

Don't simply think outside the box; realize that there is no box. Escape the confines of others and your own mind.

Most have a mansion of potential yet they are stuck in one room.

Look Your mind is even more than a mansion and you can live in more than one room then go outside! I like to go in other mansions of other individuals mind and see what in their! Explore and expand your mind.

Day 247: Theme Tuesday

The most ambitious goal in life is to be a leading conscious influence in the process of evolution. Unite with yourself and the force that runs the universe!

Therefore, think of a theme today that will aid you in this tiny tall task.

Day 248: Wisdom Wednesday

I am grateful to share how I look at life with you.

Today, you are invited to start your own unique new habit. Practice that habit for thirty-six days. If it serves you, continue it for a whole year.

> Like Tony Robbins, says, "It's not what we do once in a while that shapes our lives. It's what we do consistently."

Consistency is KING.

....

Day 249: Thankfulness Thursday

Be grateful for the small things, like safety. They often come easy, but they are the most essential. Be thankful for a safe foundation on which to build your life.

....

Day 250: Flower Friday

Gratitude is greater than love in many ways.

> "The earth smiles and laughs in flowers."
> – Ralph Waldo Emerson

If you love a flower, you don't pick it. If you pick it, it ceases to live. Love is appreciation, not ownership.

Do you love something so much that you are afraid to let it go?

···

Day 251: Stunting Saturday

Let go of showing off.

Don't make stunting a habit. Let go of that false persona you put on display. Then watch your energy power up.

When I went to nightclubs in Pittsburgh, Miami, college or of course high school! I would at times put on a show, but it drained so much of my willpower. Now I just let go, express myself, and have fun. Then I found even more energy available to put towards my vision. Stunting is bunting swing for the fences!!!

···

Day 252: Summon Thoughts Sunday

Your thoughts are amazing tools. Make time for them. Use them, but don't let them use you.

Don't think all day! Take action—the quicker the better.

> "Even if you're on the right track you'll get run over if you sit there too long." – Will Rogers

Day 253: Million Dollar Mouthpiece Monday

My friend, RSD Jeffy, and I can rapid fire and talk for hours—with passion pulsating through us.

If you are struggling with expressing yourself, eliminate judgment and just speak freely. If you can summon this super simple skill, and unwrap your gift of gab, it will serve you in more ways than one.

Day 254: Take-Me-Out Tuesday

Stare at your fear and put it on its rear. Knock it out.

Look at your problems, your challenges, and your struggles right in the eye. Knock them out.

Day 255: Wisdom Wednesday

The person that can best serve you is you.

You are only person that will always be there. You have the biggest impact on the way your life turns out.

Remember, if you are ever looking for a helping hand, all you have to do is look at the end of your own arm.

Day 256: Thankfulness Thursday

Imagine losing your freedom, being beat up, being separated from your family. These things happen all the time. Recognizing that you have many privileges and protections that others do not can help cultivate great gratitude for today.

We live in a better time now than ever. By using that colorful contrast and recognizing the enormous difference, it becomes easy to feel immense gratitude. You are living during a prosperous era and likely, in a fortunate geographical location.

Spread love today.

Day 257: Five Guys Friday

Here is quick reminder to look around you and describe the quality of people in your life.

I've said it before and by golly, I am going to say it again.

> "You are the average of the five people you spend the most time with." – Jim Rohn

How do they encourage you think, feel, and behave?

Day 258: Stick It Out Saturday

Let's give your goals your whole, not just a part. Stay sharp like a dart, show heart, and finish what you start!

Consistency, persistence, and commitment even when times get tough are paramount. The reward is worth it.

....

Day 259: Still Sunday

After a stupendous stillness session I feel super sensational. You can feel this way as well.

All you have to do is sit still for twenty minutes a day and focus on a sensory perception—a sight, a sound, a smell, or even your breath. Make one of those your anchor to the present moment now.

Spend some time doing nothing and you will notice that you are everything.

....

Day 260: Mediocrity Monday

Avoid mediocrity by motivating yourself. What does that look like for you?

Come up with three ways that you can spring into action when you are lacking motivation.

My three are:

1. Looking at my motives. Discovering my 'why's.'
2. Moving in a motivated way (jumping, running, dancing or exercising).
3. Serving and helping others.

> Andrew Carnegie said, "People who are unable to motivate themselves must be content with mediocrity no matter how impressive their talents are."

So what are you doing today to motivate yourself? or be mediocre and piss away your potential! But that's not what you are about that's why you are looking at this book because you are motivated to be your best.

••

Day 261: Team Tuesday

Teamwork makes the dream work. Do you have a support network?

Nearly every successful person that I have met has a support network.

When tough times arise—which they will—your network will be there to remind you of your awesomeness. They will help you bend, not break. Surround yourself with mentors and seek guidance from people who will support you.

••

Day 262: Wall Wednesday

Oftentimes obstacles are opportunities.

Remember to get resourceful and look at the possibilities around you. Challenges help you grow.

"If you're trying to achieve, there will be roadblocks. I've had them; everybody has had them. But obstacles don't have to stop you. If you run into a wall, don't turn around and give up. Figure out how to climb it, go through it, or work around it." – Michael Jordan

Day 263: Thankfulness Thursday

Remember a time you felt extremely grateful. Focus on it. Feel it.

How did you breathe? What did you smell? What did you hear? How did you experience it? Just visualize it for a couple seconds. Keep going!

Be grateful.

Day 264: Fire Walk Friday

"Feel the fear and do it anyway. " I once walked over two thousand hot coals, because I knew I had to confront my fear.

What fears can you trample over?

Day 265: Screw Saturday

Sometimes we think that we get screwed. The truth is we are screwing ourselves. Violate the victim mentality. Volunteer

to create change, and empower yourself to create meaning out of your challenges.

Everything that screws us—that challenges us—ends up screwing us into place. Challenges are tools to help us grow. So every time you see a screw, remember that.

Day 266: Stillness Sunday

After a long week, take some time to absorb everything, recharge, and let go.

There is success in the simplicity and sacredness of stillness.

Stop. Surrender to the now. Allow.

Space creates a place for peace and power. It doesn't have to be for an hour. Just create the space to be still.

You deserve growth and awareness wherever you are on your journey. When you pray, you speak to God, the universe or nature whatever you wish to call that animating force in the world. When you meditate, you listen. Observe and notice what is coming up inside you.

Day 267: Midas Touch Monday

Can you identify something that you can improve on? If so, spend more time immersed in doing that thing.

In your life, make it your objective to turn everything you touch into gold. Leave people, places, and things better off than how you found them.

....

Day 268: Trip Tuesday

When you explore and adventure, you'll become more aware and awestruck by your surroundings.

Find wonder and enjoyment in exploration. Take a trip to a foreign land and experience new things. It will force your brain to wake up and immerse itself in the present moment.

....

Day 269: Wisdom Wednesday

There is nothing that you cannot handle. You have made it through your whole life, and you can make it through more.

Whatever life throws at you, you will be able to cope with it. You made it this far. Now, move boldly into the future.

....

Day 270: Thankfulness Thursday

I am super duper grateful to be living with purpose—living with meaning and using my skills to help others! It was not always this way! it used to be all about just me.

I'm grateful for my current reality. However, I would not have noticed the beauty in my life without experiencing its

opposite. Life is filled with dualities and the contrast from the ups and downs give us the color for our experience

How do you cultivate thanksgiving for the tough times and who you were to wh you are now?

....

Day 271: Fun Friday

If fun is not number one, then you are missing out. Reserve a place for fun in your top ten.

In *How to Win Friends and Influence People*, Dale Carnegie said, "People rarely succeed unless they are having fun in what they are doing."

So are you having fun in what you are doing? Can you make play and fun more of a priority? Surprisingly it will boost your energy, mood, productivity and results.

....

Day 272: Spring Break Saturday

I once spent a Saturday in Fort Lauderdale with a bunch of spring breakers. They were partying and enjoying the sun.

I encourage you to celebrate everyday—not just once in awhile.

Prime yourself to be in a beautiful state as often as you can.

Day 273: Semester Sunday

Dominate, play big, and learn during every semester of the School of Life.

Life is like a series of semesters—each featuring different themes and ideas. Every season and semester is different. Be sensitive to the changes. Grow along the way and get the lessons with each one we are given.

Day 274: Moderate Monday

To lose weight, mitigate the sugar and unhealthy foods. Find a fitness plan you are fanatical about.

There are thousands of modalities. Get fit running, roller-skating, boxing, or swimming the list goes on what is it for you?

When you learn to moderate your carbs, eat mostly veggies, enough protein, avoid trans and saturated fat, and find a fitness plan that works you will be well on your way.

Day 275: Terrible Tuesday

The worst day of my life, turned out to be the best day ever.

Tough times don't last but tough people do.

We must not wait and react to life. We cannot let life happen to us. We have to make life happen.

Be proactive. Have the self-esteem to seek what you want because you are so worth it.

Day 276: Wisdom Wednesday

Remind yourself several times a day to stop, look and listen. Say those three words aloud, and give your attention to each action.

This will enable you to go from having ordinary experiences to enjoying the truth of life's adventures everyday.

Get in touch with your body and you notice incredible things that have been going unnoticed.

Day 277: Thankfulness Thursday

I am eternally grateful whenever I meet new person living with purpose and passion like me. It seems like everyday I meet a new young entrepreneur seeking to help others with their skills.

We are blessed to live in a world where we are free to do that.

Do you have a goal of starting a business?

If not now, when? If not you, who?

Day 278: Fresh People Friday

Visiting crowded places with anonymity gives you myriad of benefits. Going somewhere new and meeting new people can be an exercise of authenticity. Show them your wild side, your truth, your silliness because you may never see them again.

Socialize in abundant places as often as you can. Then watch as opportunities unfold all around you. Put yourself out there. Half of success is showing up.

Day 279: Shout Saturday

As people get older, "Life knocks the shout out of them."

Too many people go through life like zombies—walking around depressed and hopeless. They whisper when they speak.

I have compassion for them. They may be stuck in a job that they emotionally quit a long time ago but stuck with just to get by. Essentially, they let their dreams dissolve.

Determine if you are stuck by screaming at the TOP OF YOUR LUNGS. Notice if there's any blockage any resistance showing you that you may be stiffled?

Life can be painful, but don't let it knock the shout out of you. Speak loudly today.

Day 280: Savior Sunday

Sometimes we expect something or someone to come save us. To be blunt hat is bullshit. That is false hope. You will always have to save yourself first.

The glory days are here. The golden hours are now upon us and the divine timing is always this moment. It's your responsibility to be aware and enjoy the opportunities in front of you—not wait for some glorious moment down the road.

Be who you want to be, in this very moment.

....

Day 281: Man Monday

"Judge a man by his questions rather than his answers." – Voltaire

I once heard a story about a father who always asked his son what he learned in school. His son always shrugged his shoulders and said, "Nothing." That same boy had a friend whose father asked him a different question, "What did you ask in school today?" That boy always had an answer.

This story has had a profound impact on me by encouraging me to become more conscious of asking question. Now, I invite you to ask yourself and others more genuine questions so you and them can grow.

Einstein said, "Try not to become a man of success, rather become a man of value."

So how are you becoming a valuable man or woman?

Day 282: Take a Look Tuesday

You can adopt others' perspectives for a while and then go back to your own. It may make you appreciate how you see life or teach you new ways to improve your outlook.

By learning from others, you can mold a bunch of experiences and philosophies into your own worldview.

Create a colorful perspective that will serve you. Buy into other systems of living, and you will be amazed.

Day 283: Wisdom Wednesday

"You are a living magnet, what you attract into your life is in harmony with your dominant thoughts."
– Brian Tracy

Oftentimes your thoughts are products of your belief systems. You think as the person you believe you are. Therefore, today, start seeing yourself as the person you would like to be. Then adapt your behaviors to match the behaviors of the ideal version of yourself.

> Brian Tracy says, "The person we believe ourselves to be will always act in a manner consistent with our self image."

Who do you believe yourself to be? And does that serve you for what you want?

Day 284: Thankfulness Thursday

I am grateful to make another gratitude entry. I appreciate that my brain is functioning and allowing me to type this message. I'm grateful for my eyes—which allow me to read this message, and my fingers—which allow me to type it.

Be thankful for everything you have. Gratitude breeds happiness; positivity breeds success. Think about the five things you are most thankful for today.

Day 285: Foolish Friday

Amplify your audacity.
Bolster your boldness.
Cultivate your courage.

It's as easy as ABC, you see?

Pushing your limits until you are off balance has taught me many lessons. I'm grateful for those experiences. Some of the greatest icons of our eras (Steve Jobs, The Wright Brothers, etc.) were foolish. They tested their boundaries.

Test your boundaries as well. Sometimes, the best way to do that is to go too far.

••

Day 286: Self-Image Saturday

"The 'self-image' is the key to human personality and human behavior. Change the self image and you change the personality and the behavior."
– Maxwell Maltz

Acting out of alignment with the way you imagine yourself will initially cause resistance.

That is why, "A strong, positive self-image is the best possible preparation for success."
– Joyce Brothers

Be aware of the story you that you tell yourself everyday. Also, be conscious of why you tell that story. Most importantly, build on the behaviors that you plan to continue in the future aligned with the authentic you which is any positive quality you can imagine and so much more.

••

Day 287: Seeking Sunday

I'm a poet and I know it. I rhyme all the time, never looking at other people's faces. I don't wait for their reaction, or gauge their degree of satisfaction. No need to seek approval, I'm not some baby poodle. Yet still have a knack for learning and receiving feedback.

When your emotions easily fluctuate up and down, you know you are seeking validation. You are out of integrity. It's childish, obnoxious, and poisonous; avoid it like the plague.

Living your life without dependency on others reactions is living in alignment with your truth. It's a tall order, but you are worth it. you are a badass so own it.

Give yourself approval and appreciation. When you love yourself first, others will be more likely to love you as well. Like yourself before you check your likes on social media.

Day 288: Mystery Monday

> "It is through this mysterious power that we too have our being." – Sitting Bull

> "Children astound me with their inquisitive minds. The world is wide and mysterious to them, and as they piece together the puzzle of life, they ask 'Why?' ceaselessly." – John C Maxwell

Mystery can be misty, and misery can be confusing. However, mystery can also be magical. We rarely wonder anymore. We have phones and computers that answer all our questions. In the past, we would all wonder by the campfire, discussing ideas and sharing magical tales. There is power in mystery. Muster up the magic in your mind to create wondrous worlds that force you to question and explore.

As The Cheshire Cat told Alice, "If you don't know where you're going, then any road'll take you there."

"To know the road ahead, ask those coming back." Therefore, we must wonder with others. We must solve mysteries with the marvelous mentors we meet on our journey.

Day 289: There is No Competition Tuesday

Tony Robbins suggests that most people don't know what they want, don't think they can achieve it, or don't have a goal in mind. Therefore, if you do, then you are one major step ahead of them. You are statistically more likely to reach your optimal objective. Today, become crystal clear and razor sharp on your outcome.

Day 290: Wisdom Wednesday

We can choose how we can feel in each moment. You can theorize and discuss concepts all day. However, when it comes down to it, push comes to shove, what will you choose to be right now? Embody the truth of whatever you want to be.

As my mentor Elliott Hulse says, "We constantly have to make a choice about how we are going to feel. This is where it all begins."

Day 291: Thankfulness Thursday

Have you ever gone without air? How about without water?

Today, notice those gifts from God. Feel a sense of appreciation for the many small yet vital things we look past everyday like a working cardiovascular and respiratory system because someone somewhere is in the hospital for a lack of just that!!

I am grateful for the air I breathe. You ever go without breathing oxygen? Well once you stop, you will start to appreciate it.

....

Day 292: Find Friday

I'm so blessed to have met so many amazing authors, speakers, investors and incredible influencers over the past few years. While attending one event, I met with Charles Vest who sat and coached me for over half an hour. This is the lesson stuck out the most:

"Find something to fall in love with—with someone else—within the first thirty seconds." The quote is attributed to Zig Ziglar. By applying it, your networking skills will skyrocket.

Take it even deeper, be specefic find out what makes people tick—what empowers them—and connect with that.

Day 293: Statement Saturday

I once had the privilege of interviewing the Founder & Creator of Uggs boots Brian Smith for ten terrific minutes. I pulled powerful principles of success from a man who made a company worth well over a couple hundred million dollars. These are the four takeaways that you will gain the most value from:

1) FEAST upon uncertainty

2) FATTEN on Disappointment

3) ENTHUSE over apparent defeat

4) INVIGORATE in the presence of difficulties

Live these four statements and, without a shadow of a doubt, you will make a statement.

···

Day 294: Sponging Sunday

I once spoke with Jeff Hoffman the co-founder of Priceline, a company worth or made well beyond a billion dollars (yes billion with a B). what he does is deep daily *info-sponging*.

"I take time every single day to learn one new thing. You could read your journal, you could watch something new, you could check out a new website, pick up a new magazine at the store or even watch your videos Doug. Everyday, I just follow my curiosity."

By consistently coloring your creativity with different information everyday, you can expect extraordinary results.

By reading this book, you are already fertilizing your mind with creativity.

Day 295: Mentorship Monday

Get counsel over opinion.

Greg Reid, author of over fifty books, suggests that opinion is based off ignorance, lack of knowledge, and inexperience, while counsel contains wisdom, knowledge and mentorship. Always seek the latter.

> "Successful people seek council and failures listen to opinion." – John Schwartz

This one is HUGE!

Day 296: Terrific Tuesday

Can you remember the last time someone asked you how you were doing? How did you respond?

Did you say you were doing great?

I am all about generating positive energy, so my answer is almost always a resounding, "I am doing terrific!" or at least something better than good.

Feeling great will help you accomplish your goals. Spice it up and respond with interesting words from the question how are you?

142

Day 297: Wisdom Wednesday

Problems are phenomenal because they shift your perspective—allowing you to see things in a positive light. Don't mistake problems for stop signs on your road to success. They are directional guides and warning posts helping you navigate a safer and more efficient coarse. Each problem you face—each sign you pass—you gain more knowledge of the road and feel more confident navigating it.

I will gift you a sign for the rest of this book and that is FULL SPEED AHEAD!

Day 298: Thankfulness Thursday

I am so grateful to have majestic cities and metropolitan centers all over the world. At the same time, I am infinitely appreciative of the beautiful natural landscapes that compliment our urban world. Nature, in its natural essence, is the perfect contrast to human creation. We are gifted with the best of both worlds.

Day 299: Full-Out Friday

Play full out in everything you do. When athletes play in Madison Square Garden, they give their best effort. When fans come to support their teams in MSG, they cheer their loudest.

Give your best effort in everything you do, because your life is your special arena.

....

Day 300: Skip Saturday

You could skip today.

In fact, skip. Take the day off.

Just kidding. Never skip. Never quit. Be consistent, persistent, and confident in everything you do.

Relax. Reward. But never skip unless you're skipping for joy whistling toward your intentions.

....

Day 301: Someday Sunday

So many people are stuck on, "someday."

They say, "Someday, I will quit smoking."
         "Someday, I will quit my job."
         "Someday, I will start living my dream."
         "Someday, I will start working out."

If you're stuck on, "someday," let go—because, "someday," is clearly not on the calendar. You can write it on there but you will not be writing your own ticket in life. Eliminate someday from your vocabulary very fast and put it in the past.

Day 302: Macadamia Monday

Spend your life doing things you're nuts about. Talk to people about things that you are passionate about. Embark on adventures with people that get you juiced up.

If you do things you are nuts about, guess what will happen?

People will go nuts for you.

Day 303: Tank Tuesday

You are going to face many challenges and obstacles.

Run through them like a tank. Let them bounce off your hard skin, and stay in attack mode. Boom, BOOM! Vroom, vroom!!

Day 304: Wisdom Wednesday

Remain coachable and receptive even when you don't feel like it. Sometimes, you get to acknowledge that there is always room for growth and there are smarter people in the room.

Day 305: Thankfulness Thursday

I am deeply appreciative of the cornucopia of wisdom found within books, on the Internet, and within other people. What wisdom can you currently appreciate?

Day 306: Fertile Friday

A fruitful tree grows best on fertile soil. Be that tree and you are free to expand best.

Before a rocket ship blasts off into outer space, it must be entirely secure. It cannot have even the slightest chink in its armor or it will explode when it begins to leave the atmosphere. It is imperative to have a foundation built with integrity.

....

Day 307: Sick Saturday

I have not been sick in over a year. How do I manage to stay healthy for so long?

Through meditation, amazing sleep, good nutrition, and a spirited social environment.

You can do it too. I challenge you to adopt healthier habits today. Then kiss sickness goodbye. Well you may not want to kiss sickness so wave bye bye instead!

....

Day 308: Stage Sunday

> Shakespeare said, "All the world's a stage; And all the men and women merely players; They have their exits and their entrances, And one man in his time plays many parts."

What part are you playing? What stage are you on?

Day 309: Motivated Monday

"People might not get all they work for but they must certainly work for all they get." –Fredrick Douglas

How will you motivate yourself to work hard today?

Day 310: Tranquility Tuesday

"It is neither wealth nor splendor; but tranquility and occupation which gives you happiness."
– Thomas Jefferson.

Compliment your work with relaxation. What if we recharged ourselves like we did our electronics!?
Can you take a conscious inhale and deep exhale with a smile then take a great break at least twice a day?

Day 311: Wisdom Wednesday

What would you do if you knew you could not fail?

Successful people always say they wish they had started earlier. You have everything you need to start right now.

It all starts when you BELIEVE in yourself.

Day 312: Thankfulness Thursday

I deeply appreciate the privilege of living in a First World country.

I am equally as grateful to have the freedom to pursue my passions. Many countries don't offer that liberty. If you share this gift, become aware of it. Take advantage of it.

Day 313: Frontier Friday

To embark on a new frontier is to step into uncharted territory. I've been doing that a lot lately. To fuel the process of exploring the unknown, have faith in your abilities to figure things out. More importantly, have excitement, energy, and enthusiasm to make the journey as rewarding as possible.

Day 314: Steps Saturday

Bumped it to my buddy Tai Lopez watching some NBA playoffs in Omaha, Nebraska.

> He told me "Dougie Remember, when you learn from people, don't just pay attention to what they say. Pay attention to how they say it. Actions speak louder than words."

Warren Buffet who we saw that day sure does practice what he preaches.

Day 315: Secret Tip Sunday

Pester your mentors, but be polite.

Always remember to be persistent and that's with anything you want!

* * *

Day 316: Monkey Monday

If you have a monkey on your back, you can get someone else to take it off for you. However, you will limit your ability to cultivate independence.

What monkeys do you have on your back that you can take care of yourself?

Take care of them today, and you will free yourself from stress. Then let them get their on monkeys of their back if they can and most can. You can carry some people but when they drag their feet. It is ok to let some people go. Some people hold on to helping others like the monkeys hold on to their bananas and it ends up helping no one. Help yourself and put this to practice.

* * *

Day 317: Turtle Tuesday

Be like a turtle and be at ease in your own shell. However, also challenge yourself to step outside that shell at times.

Remember, slow and steady wins the race and it's great to step on the gas too!

Stay in motion, think long term and move with speed like a turtle swimming being assisted by a current in the ocean!

Day 318: Wisdom Wednesday

An old man and very successful investor once told me

"Only deal with quality people. Avoid crooks. They will drive you crazy.

Invest in people with energy, intelligence, and character".

Day 319: Thankfulness Thursday

I am grateful that I have learned from my mistakes. I grateful to fly like a dove and live with more peace and love.

Any mistakes that you are glad you had? How come?

Day 320: Fried Friday

Try to avoid fried food as often as you can.

However, make sure to fry your brain with knowledge and experience! Stretch it, challenge it, and give it space to grow.

Day 321: Shovel Saturday

Go back and dig up the past. Determine what you lack and gain that wisdom back you once had.

Today, reflect on your past experiences. Take notes on what did not work and what did. The big successes and mistakes to the small you can gather from it all! Remember, you can always learn from the past.

Day 322: Splash Sunday

When you take courageous actions, you create a ripple effect of positive IMPACT.

That ripple effect reaches out touches other areas and other people in your life. Imagine a rock being tossed into a pond or in your case you doing a cannonball from the top diving board!!

Day 323: Marathon Monday

I once watched a group of people run a twenty-seven mile marathon.

They never would have reached the finish line if they didn't know how to manage their energy. Life is a marathon. You need to know when to sprint and when to take your time. Optimize your endurance, because success is a process.

Day 324: Typical Tuesday

The best advice I have ever received was to walk away from the ninety percent.

Ninety percent of people are ordinary. I would rather be extraordinarily and abnormal.

How about you? have you joined the 10 percent of people committed to reach their potential? Of course you have and if not can you now?

....

Day 325: Wisdom Wednesday

Helen Keller was deaf and blind.

Most poetically, she said, "The only thing worse than being blind is having sight but no vision."

....

Day 326: Thankfulness Thursday

Right now, I want you to take a couple of seconds and focus on something about yourself that you are grateful for.

What do you love about yourself? Personally, I am eternally grateful for my positivity.

What are you grateful for?

Day 327: Face It Friday

Face it; you are a super fantastic, marvelous, and a magnificent treasure.

Your brilliance is founded in your ability to be you. You have so many divine gifts. Now go share them with the world. Give to be great.

Day 328: Satisfaction Saturday

You will never find lasting satisfaction in achieving your goal. Satisfaction is found when you become something more as you strive towards it. In pursuing a goal, I always become a different, more evolved person. I become a stronger version of myself.

You can too if you take action and news for you action is in satisfaction. I wish the song Satisfaction by the band the Rolling Stones mentioned that in it.

Day 329: Sweet Sunday

Wish sweet dreams to all your loved ones. Pray that they go to sleep relaxed and wake up inspired, ready to achieve their goals. You are not the only one with dreams. However, what you wish for others you seem to attract yourself.

Day 330: Master Monday

Decide to achieve mastery. Commit to learning a new skill. Persistently, playfully, passionately, and patiently work towards it. Please practice the fundamentals weekly. Be patient as you wait for the fruits of your labor.

Day 331: Toastmaster Tuesday

Do you want to improve your public speaking prowess? Do you want to enhance your communication skills and optimize your leadership potential? Then attend your local Toastmasters Club. Enjoy the process of learning in front of your peers and welcome the applause!

Day 332: Wisdom Wednesday

> Les Brown says—
> "The graveyard is the richest place on earth, because it is here that you will find all the hopes and dreams that were never fulfilled, the books that were never written, the songs that were never sung, the inventions that were never shared, the cures that were never discovered, all because someone was too afraid to take that first step, keep with the problem, or determined to carry out their dream."

So many people are afraid to take the first step. Don't let fear hold you back.

Day 333: Thankfulness Thursday

Have you ever been on airplane? How amazing is it that you can fly across the world so quickly?

I am so grateful to be able to soar amongst the clouds. We can travel through the air with food, entertainment, and even a bathroom at our disposal.

What are you grateful for?

Day 334: Fuel Friday

What fills up your tank and energizes you? What keeps you up late at night? What burns your midnight oil? What makes you pop out of bed in the morning?

Identify what fuels you and double down on it.

Day 335: Sensational Saturday

The sensational sun shines all day long without asking for anything in return. It glows—offering pure value to all of Earth's creatures.

Today, see if you can shine as bright as the sun and help your world grow.

Day 336: Strive Sunday

Don't look at your goals from a distance. Sure, somewhere far away in the night sky a star guides you on your journey. However, realize that as you work towards your goals, every single day, you are becoming something greater.

Inevitably, you will reach your destination, but don't lose sight of the treasures that you will encounter on your journey.

Day 237: Max Out Monday

Today, I want you to use up everything in your tank. Squeeze out every last drop of energy, like you would squeeze a wet towel in attempt to dry it off.

Day 338: Trusting Tuesday

You have accomplished some incredible things in your lifetime. Appreciate what you have accomplished and trust in yourself. You have the ability to overcome so many obstacles.

Day 339: Wisdom Wednesday

When your birthday rolls around, don't look at it as another year of aging. Look at it as another year of wisdom.

Every year we have amazing new experiences and learn

so much. Take what you learn and store it in your bank of wisdom then blast it all into the year ahead.

Day 340: Thankfulness Thursday

Go on a gratitude rampage. Become thankful for everything that you see. Cultivate appreciation for the fresh water you have access to, the blankets that keep you warm, and the air conditioning in your home. Be thankful for the books—which offer you knowledge, and the couch—which lets you rest.

Point it out and shout in gratitude.

Day 341: Fresh Cut Friday

Many people experience a boost of confidence after they get a haircut.

Today, attempt to cultivate confidence from within, without needing a situational trigger.

Day 342: Static Saturday

I want you to have a spark in your life! Have a thunderous purpose for living every single day. Charge yourself with electrifying energy as you work towards your passion!!!!

Day 343: Seashore Sunday

Do you find the beach relaxing? Remember, you don't have to be on the beach to experience its relaxing atmosphere. You can visit the beach in your mind through visualization.

Visualization is a powerful tool. Use it wisely. You can be wherever you want to be and feel whatever you want to feel with the power of your imagination. Albert Einstein famously said "Imagination is more powerful than knowledge"

Day 344: Measurement Monday

Take action. Notice your results. Make a record of your week. Measure your metrics and grow. Be retrospective.

> Another amazing quote Albert Einstein is attributed with saying is, "The definition of insanity is doing the same thing over and over again, but expecting different results."

We all get different results in life. Look at them objectively, get a fresh perspective, and pull lessons out of the positive and negative feedback that you receive. It can be tough on the ego, but the truth will set you free!

You cannot manage what you do not measure. Results is the name of the game.

Don't forget or neglect to reflect.

Day 345: Try It Tuesday

Try putting yourself out there. Become more vulnerable. Become more honest and humble. Connect with your humanity. When you acknowledge your imperfections, you will attract more magic into your life.

Day 346: Wisdom Wednesday

Jim Rohn said, "We all have two choices: We can make a living or we can design a life. "

He advises us to design our own life, because we only have one life to live. Have compassion for yourself as you reach for an outstanding, tailor-made life.

Day 347: Thankfulness Thursday

William Faulkner said, "Gratitude is a quality similar to electricity; it must be produced and discharged and used up in order to exist at all."

How can you produce and discharge gratitude in your life?

Day 348: Fruit Friday

Remember, every fruit on the tree is within reach. You deserve more than the low-hanging fruit. Don't settle. Set

the loftiest goals. You can achieve and reach them. Enough studying the roots climb and work for the fruit.

Day 349: Satisfied Saturday

Reward yourself every once in awhile. It's important to feel satisfied during your pursuit. With the awareness and wisdom to discern what you should relish in, you can revel in your victories and continue to make progress.

Day 350: Steam Sunday

The same laws and walls that prevent disappointment also prevent happiness. You can choose to take risks and reach for the stars. Hop off the fence already.

> Jim Rohn said, "If you are not willing to risk the unusual, you will have to settle for the ordinary."

Know that risks and pain will come with struggle, but so will happiness, growth, and connection.

Day 351: Magnificent Monday

Have you ever looked at the sky and noticed the brilliance of it? The world around you is magical. Everything that surrounds us is beautiful in its own way.

However, there is something even more magnificent inside you. It swells within and around you. Don't neglect the beauty you bring into the world. It is your Divine presence. It is your gift. Use it. Share it.

Day 352: Takeaway Tuesday

One of my biggest takeaways during my internship at the world famous Strength Camp was that so many people believed in me. Their belief in me made me believe in myself even more.

After Strength Camp, I declared I would become bolder, more passionate, confident, and enthusiastic. I gained strength and knowledge. I was taught tremendous lessons. It was an excellent experience and my greatest takeaway was that I could take what I learned and use it to propel me forward. I want to extend that confidence unto to you. Because you have picked up this book, I believe in you. Now all you have to do is believe in yourself.

Day 353: Wisdom Wednesday

Henry Ford said, "Don't find fault, find a remedy."

If you notice an area for improvement in your life, strive to fix it. Don't complain about it. Seek the remedy, today, and begin to patch up your that spot. It does not mean anything is wrong with you it is just an opportunity to enhance on your demand.

Day 354: Thankfulness Thursday

I'm grateful to have written and spoke the majority of this book. However, the chapters that I am most grateful for are the chapters of my life. Over the years, I have adopted many character virtues. One of my greatest virtues is my ability to remain teachable. It is a virtue that you too clearly share.

Remember, your life is unraveling chapter by chapter, and it is your job to take note of all the wonderful things that have already been written.

Acknowledge your commitment, consistency, growth, and receptivity. Also never compare your current chapter 4 to someone else's 24. Move next to each chapter in your life with thanks.

Day 355: Footprint Friday

The footprint that I leave on this world is of utmost importance to me. It motivates and inspires me. Beyonce has a song called "I was here" and it's my personal theme song

What imprint or impact do you want have on this world? What pumps you up and makes you take action? Identify it, begin to craft your legacy and give that song a listen.

Day 356: Sparkle Saturday

Ralph Waldo Emerson said, "Nothing great was ever achieved without enthusiasm."

Today, cultivate an enormous amount of energy. Light a scorching fire under your bum. Let that sparkle propel you towards your greatest, deepest desires with urgency and couple enjoyment toward your goal! then enthusiasm will come from within and be seen by the world.

Day 357: Sundial Sunday

A sundial depicts the time by measuring the position of the sun.

Create a sundial for your life. Know your hot spot, and know what makes you cast the largest shadow. When you discover what makes you tick, use it. It is your x-factor.

Day 358: Movie Monday

Make your life into a movie. Be your own director. Cast your own characters. Decide your own fate. Live your life with authority, and you will tell an amazing story.

Day 359: Talent Tuesday

> John Maxwell said, "Talent is a gift but character is a choice"

Remember, "Hard work beats talent when talent doesn't work hard."

••

Day 360: Wisdom Wednesday

> Jim Rohn said, "Success is not something you pursue. What you pursue will elude you. It can be like trying to chase butterflies. Success is something you attract and accumulate by the person you become."

Find ways to become a better person, there has been many in here. Act on them and you will attract success like a magnet.

••

Day 361: Thankfulness Thursday

I am thankful that struggle and negative vibes help us highlight and intensify all the good things in our lives. Recognize that the bad allows you to appreciate the good. This can be a jurassic breakthrough

What is happiness or challenges without appreciation?

Day 362: Filter Friday

Your mind has a powerful filtration system. You can filter out every undesirable person and experience in your life.

Keep all the trash out of your mind. Don't let harmful chemicals in. However, use the right tools to keep out the weeds.

Raise your standard and live a more positive, drama-free life. With a proper filtration system, the garden of your mind will grow bountiful fruits.

Day 363: Should Saturday

I want you to turn your *shoulds* into *musts*. When you do so, you will manifest a sudden shift that drastically, dramatically enhances your ability to absolutely produce extraordinary results.

When one *should* do something, you might get it done. When one *must* do something, they WILL get it done and find a way through hell or high water.

Day 364: So Close Sunday

Sometimes, when we approach the finish line, we self-sabotage and quit or just want to sprint ahead. Remember, the journey not done until it all ends, so keep enjoying it until your life ends. Yet, what if you lived life like it was always the

end? played like it was the 4th quarter more regularly? What would life look like for you then?

....

Day 365: Momentous Monday

The funny thing about life is when you refuse to accept anything but the absolute best, then that is exactly what you will get.

Today is the last day of our journey. Over the last year, you have taken the time to absorb these powerful daily reminders, and you have chosen to implement these strategies to enhance your quality of life. Tomorrow, when the new week begins, take the time to be appreciative of that.

However, today, recognize that you deserve the absolute best. This is your life, and by using this book you have fertilized your mind with amazing wisdom.

To bring it full circle with all this power at your fingertips, make motivated a new way of being for you, step into the light, and put your stamp on the world.

THE DESTINATION

For you to decide…

And now you have a tool to get more motivated and instantly inspired like a light bulb being turned on by your hand flicking the light switch. All we are blessed to do is realize what day it is.

ACKNOWLEDGMENTS

Editors:

Sal Marotta
Cedar Hansen
Damon Bingman
Nick Fuzzer
Ben Hirons
Carlos F. Ocon

I would like to extend my gratitude to all those that were open and inspired enough to be featured in any of the content I've ever created. I also appreciate those who were willing to hold the camera as I filmed these inspirational videos.

Also Instagram for the platform. Apple for the IPhone and Verizon for the data.

Deep gratitude for mentors in my life such as:

Luke Faust
Leslie Stenger
Joe Martin
Steven Rowell
Elliott Hulse
Chris Barnard
Mark Dhamma
Mike Straumietis
Owen Cook

Eli Wilhide
Troy Casey
Larry Benet
Lewis Howes
Chris Bolger
Joe Henderson
Chris Hawker
Brandon Carter
Yahya Bakkar
Tai Lopez
Zedrick Clark
Damon Bingman

(Yes I have a ton of mentors. Nobody succeeds alone and my next book will be on mentorship!!)

Also a BIG thanks to the Angels in my life such as, Ryan Clarkin, Jairek Robbins, Julian Bradley, Farhan Khawaja, Andrew Colombini and Brittany Revels.

To be honest everyone is an angel in our lives, a mirror and crystal ball if we choose to see their blessings. Elliott Hulse taught me that and you can see him speak about that with this link: https://youtu.be/wsbE9j6U5R0

Deepest thanks to my Family:

Father Joe Forlano
Big Brother Taylor Forlano
Mother Wendy Forlano
Sister Melody Forlano

FOR MORE DAILY INSPIRATIONAL CONTENT...

You can watch all of these entries in the supporting environment on video originally created on Instagram at Dougiefresh44

invite you to go now and back track to see, hear and feel them yourself.

YouTube: Dougie Forlano

Snap chat: Dougieblessed44

Facebook: Dougie Forlano

THANKS FOR READING!

Please leave a review!

Made in the USA
Lexington, KY
23 July 2018